THIMBLEBERRIES®

Quilting for Harvest

Landauer Books

This book was designed, produced, and published by Landauer Books
A division of Landauer Corporation
3100 NW 101st Street, Urbandale, Iowa 50322
www.landauercorp.com

President: Jeramy Lanigan Landauer
Editor-in-Chief: Becky Johnston
Art Director: Laurel Albright
Creative Director: Lynette Jensen
Photographers: Craig Anderson and Dennis Kennedy
Photostyling: Lynette Jensen
Technical Writer: Sue Bahr
Technical Illustrator: Lisa Kirchoff

We also wish to thank the support staff of the
Thimbleberries® Design Studio: Sherry Husske, Virginia Brodd,
Renae Ashwill, Ardelle Paulson, Kathy Lobeck, Carla Wegner,
Julie Jergens, Pearl Baysinger, Tracy Schrantz,
Amy Albrecht, Leone Rusch, and Julie Borg.

The following manufacturers are licensed to sell Thimbleberries®
products: Thimbleberries® Rugs (www.colonialmills.com);
Thimbleberries® Quilt Stencils (www.quiltingcreations.com); and
Thimbleberries® Sewing Thread (www.robison-anton.com).

This book is printed on acid-free paper.

Printed in China 10 9 8 7 6 5 4 3 2 1

Library of Congress Cataloging-in-Publication Data
available on request.

ISBN 10: 1-890621-16-1

ISBN 13: 978-1-890621-16-2

Contents

Introduction

Autumn comes early to Minnesota where I live. The golden hues of the last leaves of summer lingering on the towering trees surrounding my home inspire many of the quilts I design for Thimbleberries®. September ushers in autumn with the crisp scent of cool mornings that warm to sunny afternoons—just right for gathering nature's abundant harvest. October is nature's paintbrush, gilding my doorstep with intense colors— from toasty brown to goldenrod. And November is the season to be thankful for peace and plenty. I hope you enjoy the special pleasures of autumn and quilting for harvest as much as I do.

My best,

Lynette Jensen

Pumpkin Picking

A scattering of leaves and a sturdy pumpkin combine for a welcoming quilted wall display.

Wall Quilt

36 x 42-inches

Fabrics & Supplies

1/2 yard	**PUMPKIN PRINT** for pumpkin and inner border
3/4 yard	**BEIGE LEAF PRINT** for background
1/3 yard	**GREEN MOSS PRINT** for pumpkin stem, leaf blocks, and quilt center
1/8 yard	**BROWN LEAF PRINT** for leaf blocks
1/8 yard	**BROWN FLORAL** for leaf blocks
3/4 yard	**GREEN LEAF PRINT** for outer border
1/3 yard	**BROWN PRINT** for quilt center
1/2 yard	**PUMPKIN PRINT** for binding

1-3/8 yards for backing

quilt batting, at least 42 x 48-inches

NOTE: read **Getting Started**, page 123, before beginning this project.

Pumpkin Block

Cutting

From **PUMPKIN PRINT**:
- Cut 1, 6-1/2 x 42-inch strip. From the strip cut: 2, 6-1/2 x 12-1/2-inch rectangles

From **BEIGE LEAF PRINT**:
- Cut 1, 4-1/2 x 42-inch strip. From the strip cut:
  1, 4-1/2 x 6-1/2-inch rectangle
  1, 4-1/2-inch square
  1, 2-1/2 x 12-1/2-inch rectangle
  6, 2-1/2-inch squares
  2, 1-1/2-inch squares

From **GREEN MOSS PRINT**:
- Cut 1, 2-1/2 x 42-inch strip. From the strip cut:
  1, 2-1/2 x 12-1/2-inch rectangle (to be used in the Quilt Center Section—set aside)
  1, 2-1/2 x 4-1/2-inch rectangle
  2, 2-1/2-inch squares

Piecing

Step 1   With right sides together, position a 2-1/2-inch **BEIGE** square on the upper and lower left corners of a 6-1/2 x 12-1/2-inch **PUMPKIN** rectangle. Draw a diagonal line on the squares and stitch on the lines. Trim the seam allowances to 1/4-inch; press. Repeat this process at the lower right corner of the rectangle using a 1-1/2-inch **BEIGE** square.

Make 1

Step 2 With right sides together, position a 2-1/2-inch **BEIGE** square on the upper and lower right corners of the remaining 6-1/2 x 12-1/2-inch **PUMPKIN** rectangle. Draw a diagonal line on the squares; stitch, trim, and press. Repeat this process at the upper left corner of the rectangle using a 2-1/2-inch **GREEN MOSS PRINT** square, and at the lower left corner using a 1-1/2-inch **BEIGE** square.

Make 1

Step 3 Sew the Step 1 and Step 2 units together; press. <u>At this point the unit should measure 12-1/2-inches square.</u>

Make 1

Step 4 With right sides together, position a 2-1/2-inch **BEIGE** square on the corner of a 2-1/2 x 4-1/2-inch **GREEN MOSS PRINT** rectangle. Draw a diagonal line on the square; stitch, trim, and press. Repeat this process at the opposite corner of the rectangle.

Make 1

Step 5 With right sides together, position a 2-1/2-inch **GREEN MOSS PRINT** square on the lower left corner of the 4-1/2 x 6-1/2-inch **BEIGE** rectangle. Draw a diagonal line on the square; stitch, trim, and press.

Make 1

Step 6 Sew together the Step 4 and Step 5 units. Sew the 4-1/2-inch **BEIGE** square to the left edge of the unit; press. <u>At this point the stem unit should measure 4-1/2 x 12-1/2-inches.</u> Sew the stem unit to the top edge of the pumpkin unit and sew the 2-1/2 x 12-1/2-inch **BEIGE** rectangle to the bottom edge of the pumpkin unit; press. <u>At this point the pumpkin block should measure 12-1/2 x 18-1/2-inches.</u>

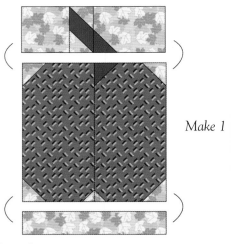

Make 1

Leaf Blocks

Makes a total of 6 blocks (2 blocks using 3 fabrics)

Cutting

From *each* **BROWN LEAF PRINT, GREEN MOSS PRINT,** and **BROWN FLORAL:**
- Cut 1, 2-7/8 x 42-inch strip. From the strip cut:
  1, 2-7/8-inch square
  2, 2-1/2 x 6-1/2-inch rectangles
  4, 2-1/2 x 4-1/2-inch rectangles
  2, 1 x 5-inch strips

From **BEIGE LEAF PRINT:**
- Cut 1, 2-7/8 x 42-inch strip. From the strip cut:
  3, 2-7/8-inch squares
  6, 2-5/8-inch squares. Cut the squares in half diagonally.
- Cut 2, 2-1/2 x 42-inch strips. From the strips cut:
  18, 2-1/2-inch squares

Piecing

Note: *The following instructions are for 2 **BROWN LEAF PRINT** leaf blocks. Repeat these steps to make 2 **GREEN MOSS PRINT** leaf blocks and 2 **BROWN FLORAL LEAF** blocks.*

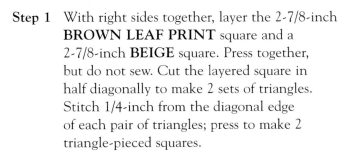

Step 1 With right sides together, layer the 2-7/8-inch **BROWN LEAF PRINT** square and a 2-7/8-inch **BEIGE** square. Press together, but do not sew. Cut the layered square in half diagonally to make 2 sets of triangles. Stitch 1/4-inch from the diagonal edge of each pair of triangles; press to make 2 triangle-pieced squares.

   Make 2, 2-1/2-inch triangle-pieced squares

Step 2 With right sides together, position a 2-1/2-inch **BEIGE** square on the right corner of a 2-1/2 x 4-1/2-inch **BROWN LEAF PRINT** rectangle. Draw a diagonal line on the square; stitch, trim, and press. Make 4 units. Sew a triangle-pieced square to the right edge of 2 of the units; press.

Make 4   *Make 2*

Step 3 With right sides together, position a 2-1/2-inch **BEIGE** square on the left corner of a 2-1/2 x 6-1/2-inch **BROWN LEAF PRINT** rectangle. Draw a diagonal line on the square; stitch, trim, and press.

Make 2

Step 4 To make a stem unit, center a **BEIGE** triangle on a 1 x 5-inch **BROWN LEAF PRINT** strip; stitch with a 1/4-inch seam allowance. Center another **BEIGE** triangle on the opposite edge of the **BROWN LEAF PRINT** strip; stitch and trim. Make 2 stem units. Sew the remaining Step 2 units to the left edge of each stem unit; press.

Trim ends

Make 2 stem units

Make 2

Step 5 Lay out the leaf units, sew together; press. At this point each leaf block should measure 6-1/2-inches square.

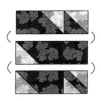

Make 2 BROWN LEAF PRINT blocks

Step 6 Repeat Steps 1 through 5 to make the remaining leaf blocks.

Make 2 GREEN MOSS blocks   *Make 2 BROWN FLORAL blocks*

Step 7 Sew the leaf blocks together in 2 strips of 3 leaf blocks each; press. At this point the leaf strips should measure 6-1/2 x 18-1/2-inches.

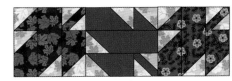

Make 2

Quilt Center

Cutting

From **BROWN PRINT:**
- Cut 2, 4-1/2 x 42-inch strip. From the strip cut: 4, 4-1/2 x 12-1/2-inch rectangles

From **GREEN MOSS PRINT:**
- Cut 1, 2-1/2 x 42-inch strip. From the strip cut: 3, 2-1/2 x 12-1/2-inch rectangles (1 additional rectangle was cut in the Pumpkin Block Section)

From **BEIGE LEAF PRINT:**
- Cut 2, 6-1/2 x 42-inch strips. From the strips cut: 8, 6-1/2-inch squares

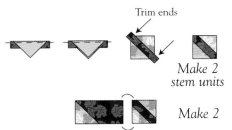

Quilt Center Assembly

Step 1 Aligning long edges, sew together the 2-1/2 x 12-1/2-inch **GREEN MOSS PRINT** rectangles and the 4-1/2 x 12-1/2-inch **BROWN PRINT** rectangles in pairs; press.

Make 4

Step 2 With right sides together, position a 6-1/2-inch **BEIGE** square on the corner of a Step 1 rectangle. Draw a diagonal line on the square; stitch, trim, and press. Repeat this process at the opposite corner of the unit. Make 4 units. Sew the units together in pairs; press. <u>At this point each section should measure 6-1/2 x 24-1/2-inches.</u>

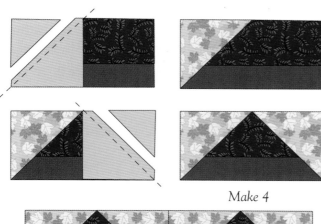

Make 4

Make 2

Step 3 Refer to the quilt assembly diagram and sew the sections together; press. <u>At this point the quilt center should measure 24-1/2 x 30-1/2-inches.</u>

Quilt Assembly Diagram

Borders

Note: *The yardage given allows for the border strips to be cut on the crosswise grain. Diagonally piece the strips as needed, referring to* **Diagonal Piecing** *instructions on page 128. Read through* **Border** *instructions on pages 127–128 for general instructions on adding borders.*

Cutting

From **PUMPKIN PRINT:**
* Cut 4, 1-1/2 x 42-inch inner border strips

From **GREEN LEAF PRINT**:
* Cut 4, 5-1/2 x 42-inch outer border strips

Attaching the Borders

Step 1 Attach the 1-1/2-inch wide **PUMPKIN PRINT** inner border strips.

Step 2 Attach the 5-1/2-inch wide **GREEN LEAF PRINT** outer border strips.

Putting It All Together

Trim the backing and batting so they are 6-inches larger than the quilt top. Refer to **Finishing The Quilt** on page 128 for complete instructions.

Binding

Cutting

From **PUMPKIN PRINT**:

• Cut 5, 2-3/4 x 42-inch strips

Sew the binding to the quilt using a 3/8-inch seam allowance. This measurement will produce a 1/2-inch wide finished double binding. Refer to **Binding** and **Diagonal Piecing** on page 128 for complete instructions.

Pumpkin Picking Wall Quilt
36 x 42-inches

Harvest Leaf

Herald the onset of autumn with a harvest of leaves—an inviting wrap-up for cool evenings.

Throw

65 x 76-1/4-inches

Fabrics & Supplies

1-1/3 yards	**TAN PRINT** for appliqué foundation squares
1-1/4 yards	**GREEN PRINT** for leaf appliqués
7/8 yard	**HALLOWEEN SIGNATURE PRINT** for alternate blocks
7/8 yard	**ORANGE FLORAL** for side and corner triangles
1 yard	**BLACK PRINT** for inner border and second middle border
1-5/8 yards	**ORANGE PUMPKIN PRINT** for first middle border and outer border
3/4 yard	**BLACK PRINT** for binding

4 yards for backing

quilt batting, at least 71 x 83-inches

template material

paper-backed fusible web for appliqués

pearl cotton or machine embroidery thread for decorative stitches: black

tear-away fabric stabilizer (optional)

NOTE: read **Getting Started**, page 123, before beginning this project.

Appliqué - Fusible Web Method

Cutting

From **TAN PRINT:**

- Cut 5, 8-1/2 x 42-inch strips.
  From the strips cut:
  20, 8-1/2-inch appliqué foundation squares

Step 1 Make a template of the appliqué shape on page 17. Trace 20 leaf shapes onto the paper side of the fusible web, leaving a small margin between each shape. Cut the shapes apart.

Step 2 Following the manufacturer's instructions, fuse the shapes to the wrong side of the fabric chosen for the appliqués. Let the fabric cool and cut along the traced line. Peel away the paper backing from the fusible web.

Step 3 Referring to the quilt diagram, position the appliqué shapes on the 8-1/2-inch **TAN** appliqué foundation squares; fuse in place. We suggest pinning a rectangle of tear-away stabilizer to the backside of the fabric to be appliquéd on so that it will lay flat when the appliqué is complete. We use the extra-lightweight Easy Tear™ sheets as a stabilizer. When the appliqué is complete, tear away the stabilizer.

Step 4 We machine blanket stitched around the shapes using black machine embroidery thread for the top thread and regular sewing thread in the bobbin. If you like, you could hand-blanket stitch around the shapes with pearl cotton.

Blanket Stitch

Note: To prevent the hand-blanket stitches from "rolling off" the edges of the appliqué shapes, take an extra back-stitch in the same place as you made the blanket stitch, going around outer curves, corners, and points. For straight edges, taking a backstitch every inch is enough.

Quilt Center

Note: The side and corner triangles are larger than necessary and will be trimmed before the borders are added.

Cutting

From HALLOWEEN SIGNATURE PRINT:
- Cut 3, 8-1/2 x 42-inch strips. From the strips cut: 12, 8-1/2-inch alternate block squares

From ORANGE FLORAL:
- Cut 2, 13 x 42-inch strips. From the strips cut: 4, 13-inch squares. Cut the squares diagonally into quarters to make 16 triangles. You will be using only 14 for side triangles.
  2, 8-inch squares. Cut the squares in half diagonally to make 4 corner triangles.

Quilt Center Assembly

Step 1 Referring to the quilt diagram for block placement, sew together the appliquéd blocks, the **HALLOWEEN SIGNATURE PRINT** alternate blocks, and the **ORANGE FLORAL** side triangles in 8 diagonal rows. Press the seam allowances toward the alternate blocks and side triangles.

Step 2 Pin the block rows together at the block intersections and sew the rows together. Press the seam allowances in one direction.

Step 3 Sew the **ORANGE FLORAL** corner triangles to the quilt center; press.

Step 4 Trim away the excess fabric from the side and corner triangles taking care to allow a 1/4-inch seam allowance beyond the corners of each block. Read through **Trimming Side and Corner Triangles** below for complete instructions.

Trimming Side and Corner Triangles

Begin at a corner by lining up your ruler 1/4-inch beyond the points of the corners of the blocks as shown.
Cut along the edge of the ruler. Repeat this procedure on all four sides of the quilt top.

Trim to 1/4"

1/4" seam allowance

Make sure the corners are 90° angles before you cut

1/4" seam allowance

Borders

*Note: The yardage given allows for the border strips to be cut on the crosswise grain. Diagonally piece the strips as needed, referring to **Diagonal Piecing** instructions on page 128. Read through **Border** instructions on pages 127–128 for general instructions on adding borders.*

Cutting

From BLACK PRINT:
- Cut 6, 2-1/2 x 42-inch inner border strips
- Cut 7, 2-1/2 x 42-inch second middle border strips

From ORANGE PUMPKIN PRINT:
- Cut 8, 4-1/2 x 42-inch outer border strips
- Cut 7, 2-1/2 x 42-inch first middle border strips

Attaching the Borders

Step 1 Attach the 2-1/2-inch wide **BLACK** inner border strips.

Step 2 Attach the 2-1/2-inch wide **ORANGE PUMPKIN PRINT** first middle border strips.

Step 3 Attach the 2-1/2-inch wide **BLACK** second middle border strips.

Step 4 Attach the 4-1/2-inch wide **ORANGE PUMPKIN** print outer border strips.

Putting It All Together

Cut the 4 yard length of backing fabric in half crosswise to make 2, 2 yard lengths. Refer to **Finishing the Quilt** on page 128 for complete instructions.

Binding

Cutting

From **BLACK PRINT**:
- Cut 8, 2-3/4 x 42-inch strips

Sew the binding to the quilt using a 3/8-inch seam allowance. This measurement will produce a 1/2-inch wide finished double binding. Refer to **Binding** and **Diagonal Piecing** on page 128 for complete instructions.

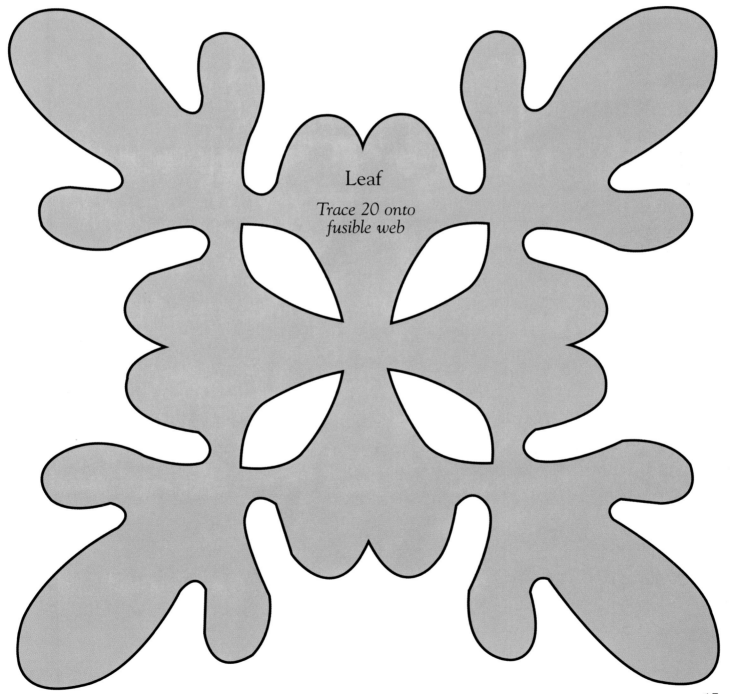

Leaf

Trace 20 onto fusible web

Harvest Leaf Throw
65 x 76-1/4-inches

Celebrate autumn with a dramatic layering of leaves and pumpkins using vintage ironwork transformed into a tiered plant stand.

Picnic Potluck

For an easy autumn treat, serve up a generous helping of apple slices topped with caramel and pecans.

uilt

58 x 68-inches

Fabrics & Supplies

1/8 yard	**each** of 20 ASSORTED DARK PRINTS for blocks *(or a total of 1-5/8 yards)*
1-1/2 yards	BEIGE PRINT for background
1-1/8 yards	BLACK PRINT for lattice and inner border
1/2 yard	GREEN PRINT #1 for middle border
1-1/2 yards	GOLD w/RED LEAF PRINT for outer border
5/8 yard	GREEN PRINT #2 for binding

3-1/2 yards for backing

quilt batting, at least 62 x 72-inches

*NOTE: read **Getting Started**, page 123, before beginning this project.*

Pieced Blocks

Makes 20 blocks

Cutting

From **each** of the **20 ASSORTED DARK PRINTS:**
- Cut 1, 2-1/2 x 42-inch strip. From each strip cut: 8, 2-1/2 x 4-1/2-inch rectangles *(or a total of 160, 2-1/2 x 4-1/2-inch rectangles)*

From **BEIGE PRINT:**
- Cut 20, 2-1/2 x 42-inch strips. From the strips cut: 320, 2-1/2-inch squares

Piecing

Step 1 With right sides together, position a 2-1/2-inch **BEIGE** square on the corner of a 2-1/2 x 4-1/2-inch **ASSORTED DARK PRINT** rectangle. Draw a diagonal line on the square and stitch on the line. Trim the seam allowance to 1/4-inch; press. Repeat this process at the opposite corner of the rectangle. <u>At this point each unit should measure 2-1/2 x 4-1/2-inches.</u>

Make 160

Step 2 Sew the Step 1 units together in pairs; press.

Make 80

Step 3 Referring to the block diagram, sew the Step 2 units together; press. <u>At this point each block should measure 8-1/2-inches square.</u>

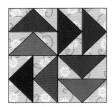

Make 20

Quilt Center

Cutting

From **BLACK PRINT:**
- Cut 4, 2-1/2 x 42-inch strips. From the strips cut: 15, 2-1/2 x 8-1/2-inch lattice segments
- Cut 6 more 2-1/2 x 42-inch strips. From the strips cut: 6, 2-1/2 x 38-1/2-inch lattice/inner border strips

Quilt Center Assembly

Step 1 Referring to the quilt diagram for block placement, sew together the pieced blocks and the 2-1/2 x 8-1/2-inch **BLACK** lattice segments to make 5 block rows; press. <u>At this point each block row should measure 8-1/2 x 38-1/2-inches.</u>

Step 2 Pin the block rows and 2-1/2 x 38-1/2-inch **BLACK** lattice strips together; sew. Press the seam allowances toward the lattice strips.

Borders

Note: *The yardage given allows for the border strips to be cut on the crosswise grain. Diagonally piece the strips as needed, referring to* **Diagonal Piecing** *instructions on page 128. Read through* **Border** *instructions on pages 127–128 for general instructions on adding borders.*

Cutting

From **BLACK PRINT:**
- Cut 3, 2-1/2 x 42-inch side inner border strips

From **GREEN PRINT #2:**
- Cut 5, 2-1/2 x 42-inch middle border strips

From **GOLD w/RED LEAF PRINT:**
- Cut 7, 6-1/2 x 42-inch outer border strips

Attaching the Borders

Step 1 Attach the 2-1/2-inch wide **BLACK** side inner border strips.

Step 2 Attach the 2-1/2-inch wide **GREEN #2** middle border strips.

Step 3 Attach the 6-1/2-inch wide **GOLD w/RED LEAF PRINT** outer border strips.

Putting It All Together

Cut the 3-1/2 yard length of backing fabric in half crosswise to make 2, 1-3/4 yard lengths. Refer to **Finishing the Quilt** on page 128 for complete instructions.

Binding

Cutting

From **GREEN PRINT #2:**
- Cut 7, 2-3/4 x 42-inch strips

Sew the binding to the quilt using a 3/8-inch seam allowance. This measurement will produce a 1/2-inch wide finished double binding. Refer to **Binding** and **Diagonal Piecing** on page 128 for complete instructions.

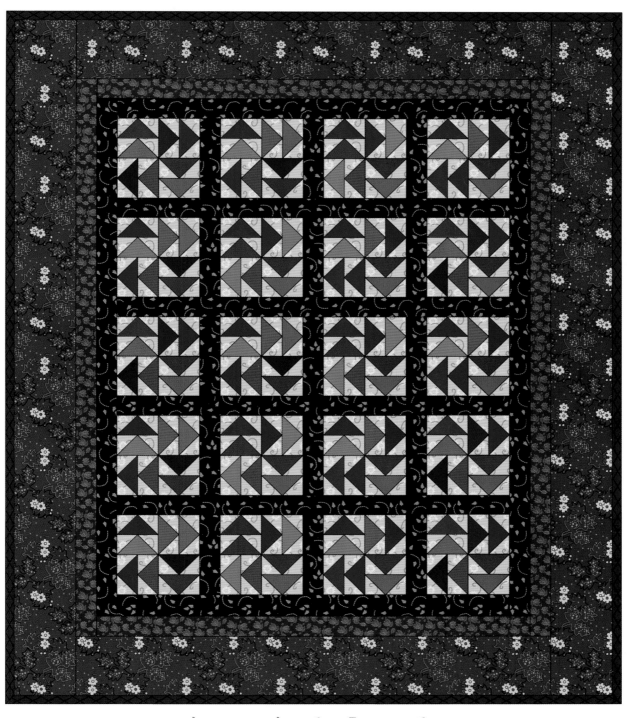

Picnic Potluck Quilt
56 x 68-inches

Autumn Splendor

Complement a harvest table topper with a potpourri of miniature Indian corn and strawflower blossoms.

Table Topper
28 x 52-inches
Fabrics & Supplies

1/2 yard	**BROWN PRINT #1** for nine-patch blocks
3/8 yard	**BEIGE PRINT #1** for nine-patch blocks
1/2 yard	**BEIGE PRINT #2** for appliqué foundation
1/4 yard	**GREEN PRINT #1** for inner border and pumpkin stem appliqués
5/8 yard	**LARGE BROWN/TAN FLORAL** for outer border
1/4 yard	**BROWN PRINT #2** for sunflower petal appliqués
1/4 yard	**GREEN PRINT #2** for sunflower center and bird appliqués
4-1/2 x 6-inch piece	**RED PRINT** for berry appliqués (bird and leaf blocks)
1/8 yard	**TAN/GREEN PRINT** for stem (bird blocks) and leaf appliqués
6 x 12-inch piece	**ORANGE PRINT** for pumpkin appliqués
1/2 yard	**GREEN PRINT #1** for binding

1-5/8 yards for backing

quilt batting, at least 36 x 58-inches

paper-backed fusible web for appliqués

lightweight cardboard for templates

machine embroidery thread or pearl cotton for decorative stitches: black

tear-away fabric stabilizer (optional)

*NOTE: read **Getting Started**, page 123, before beginning this project.*

Nine-Patch Blocks

Makes 11 blocks

Cutting

From **BROWN PRINT #1**:
- Cut 5, 2-1/2 x 42-inch strips

From **BEIGE PRINT #1**:
- Cut 4, 2-1/2 x 42-inch strips

Note: *The nine-patch blocks are made up of strip sets. Refer to page 127 for **Hints and Helps for Pressing Strips Sets**.*

Piecing

Step 1 Sew a 2-1/2 x 42-inch **BROWN #1** strip to both side edges of a 2-1/2 x 42-inch **BEIGE #1** strip; press. Make 2 strip sets. Cut the strip sets into segments.

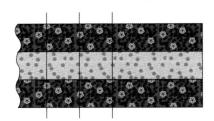

Crosscut 22, 2-1/2-inch wide segments

Step 2 Sew a 2-1/2 x 42-inch **BEIGE #1** strip to both side edges of a 2-1/2 x 42-inch **BROWN #1** strip; press. Cut the strip set into segments.

Crosscut 11, 2-1/2-inch wide segments

Step 3 Sew Step 1 segments to both side edges of the Step 2 segments; press. <u>At this point each nine-patch block should measure 6-1/2-inches square.</u>

Make 11

Appliqué Blocks - Fusible Web Method

Note: *This appliqué method was used for all the appliqué shapes with the exception of the sunflower center. The sunflower center was appliquéd using the cardboard appliqué method.*

Makes 10 blocks

Cutting

From **BEIGE PRINT #2:**

• Cut 2, 6-1/2 x 42-inch strips. From the strips cut: 10, 6-1/2-inch appliqué foundation squares

Step 1 Position the fusible web (paper side up) over the appliqué shapes on page 29. With a pencil, trace the shapes the number of times indicated on each pattern, leaving a small margin between each shape. Cut the shapes apart.

Note: *When you are fusing a large shape, like the flower, fuse just the outer edges of the shape so that it will not look stiff when finished. To do this, draw a line about 3/8-inch inside the flower, and cut away the fusible web on this line.*

Step 2 Following the manufacturer's instructions, fuse the shapes to the wrong side of the fabrics chosen for the appliqués. Let the fabric

cool and cut along the traced line of each shape. Peel away the paper backing from the fusible web.

Step 3 Referring to the quilt diagram, position the appliqué shapes on each 6-1/2-inch appliqué foundation square, layering them as needed; fuse in place. We suggest pinning a rectangle of tear-away fabric stabilizer to the backside of the appliqué foundation square so it will lay flat when the appliqué is complete. We use the extra-lightweight Easy Tear™ sheets as a stabilizer. When the appliqué is complete, tear away the stabilizer.

Step 4 Machine blanket stitch around the shapes with black embroidery thread for the top thread and regular sewing thread in the bobbin. If you like you could hand blanket stitch around the shapes with pearl cotton.

Blanket stitch

Note: *To prevent the blanket stitches from "rolling off" the edges of the appliqué shapes, take an extra backstitch in the same place as you made the blanket stitch, going around outer curves, corners, and points. For straight edges, taking a backstitch every inch is enough.*

Flower Center Appliqué - Cardboard Method

Step 1 Make a cardboard template using the flower center pattern on page 28.

Step 2 Position the template on the wrong side of the fabric chosen for the flower center, trace around the template 3 times leaving a 3/4-inch margin around each shape. Remove the template and cut a scant 1/4-inch beyond the drawn lines.

Step 3 To create smooth, round circles, run a line of basting stitches around the circle, placing the stitches halfway between the drawn line and the cut edge of the circle. After basting, keep the needle and thread attached for the next step.

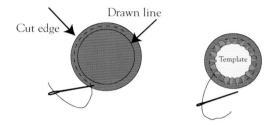
Drawn line
Cut edge
Template

Step 4 Place the cardboard template on the wrong side of a fabric circle and tug on the basting stitches, gathering the fabric over the template. When the thread is tight, space the gathers evenly, and make a knot to secure the thread. Clip the thread, press the circle, and remove the cardboard template. Make 3 flower centers.

Step 5 Referring to the quilt diagram, pin the flower centers to the sunflowers and hand appliqué in place using matching thread.

Quilt Center

Step 1 Referring to the quilt diagram for block placement, sew the nine-patch blocks and the appliquéd blocks together in 7 vertical rows of 3 blocks each. Press the seam allowances in alternating directions by rows so the seams will fit snugly together with less bulk.

Step 2 Pin the rows at the block intersections; sew the rows together. Press the seam allowances in one direction.

Borders

Note: *The yardage given allows for the border strips to be cut on the crosswise grain. Diagonally piece the strips as needed, referring to* **Diagonal Piecing** *instructions on page 128. Read through* **Border** *instructions on pages 127–128 for general instructions on adding borders.*

Cutting

From **GREEN PRINT #1:**
• Cut 4, 1-1/2 x 42-inch inner border strips

From **LARGE BROWN/TAN FLORAL:**
• Cut 4, 4-1/2 x 42-inch outer border strips

Attaching the Borders

Step 1 Attach the 1-1/2-inch wide **GREEN #1** inner border strips.

Step 2 Attach the 4-1/2-inch wide **LARGE BROWN/TAN FLORAL** outer border strips.

Putting It All Together

Trim the batting and backing so they are 6-inches larger than the quilt top. Refer to **Finishing the Quilt** on page 128 for complete instructions.

Binding

Cutting

From **GREEN PRINT #1:**
• Cut 5, 2-3/4 x 42-inch strips

Sew the binding to the quilt using a 3/8-inch seam allowance. This measurement will produce a 1/2-inch wide finished double binding. Refer to **Binding and Diagonal Piecing** page 128 for complete instructions.

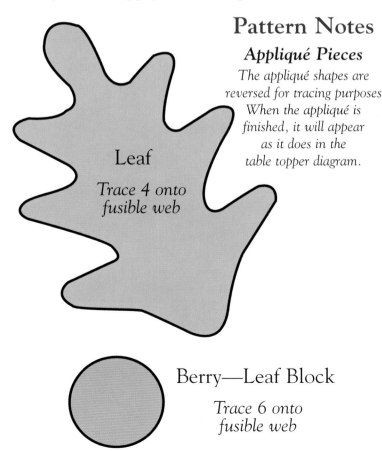

Pattern Notes

Appliqué Pieces

The appliqué shapes are reversed for tracing purposes When the appliqué is finished, it will appear as it does in the table topper diagram.

Leaf

Trace 4 onto fusible web

Berry—Leaf Block

Trace 6 onto fusible web

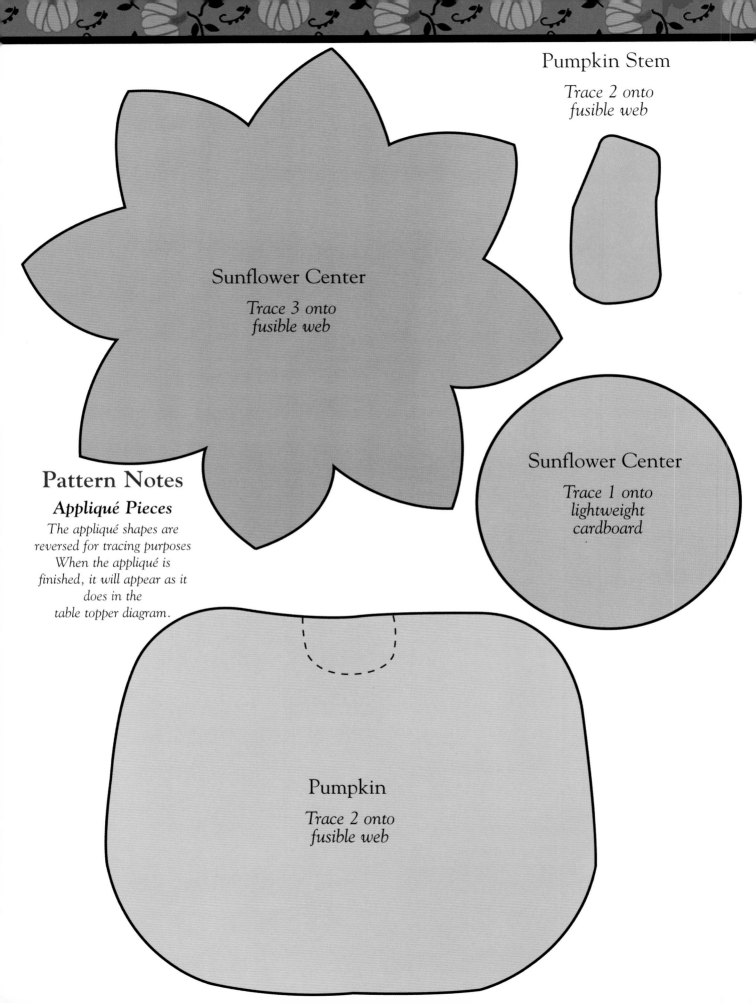

Pumpkin Stem

Trace 2 onto
fusible web

Sunflower Center

Trace 3 onto
fusible web

Sunflower Center

Trace 1 onto
lightweight
cardboard

Pattern Notes

Appliqué Pieces

The appliqué shapes are
reversed for tracing purposes
When the appliqué is
finished, it will appear as it
does in the
table topper diagram.

Pumpkin

Trace 2 onto
fusible web

Pattern Notes

Appliqué Pieces

The appliqué shapes are reversed for tracing purposes When the appliqué is finished, it will appear as it does in the table topper diagram.

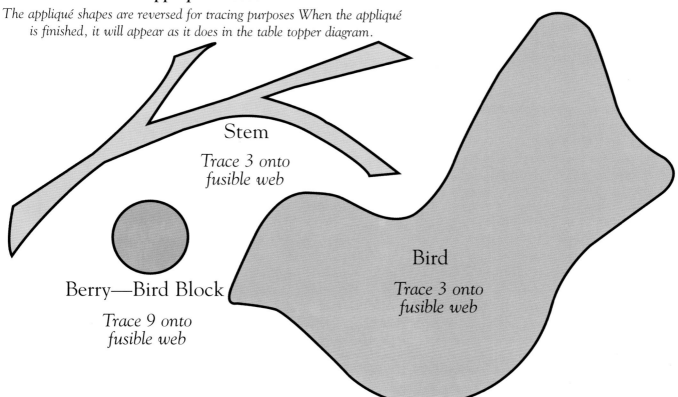

Stem

Trace 3 onto
fusible web

Berry—Bird Block

Trace 9 onto
fusible web

Bird

Trace 3 onto
fusible web

Autumn Splendor Table Topper
28 x 52-inches

Harvest Log Cabin

Make good use of the mellow warmth of brown in a rustic quilt and birdhouse display.

64 x 80-inches

Fabrics & Supplies

1/2 yard	**GOLD PRINT** for center squares
3/8 yard	*each* of 18 **ASSORTED DARK PRINTS** for Log Cabin blocks
5/8 yard	*each* of 7 **ASSORTED BEIGE PRINTS** for Log Cabin blocks
3/4 yard	**BLACK PRINT** for binding

4-3/4 yards for backing

quilt batting, at least 70 x 86-inches

NOTE: *read* **Getting Started**, *page 123, before beginning this project.*

Log Cabin Blocks

Makes 80 blocks

Cutting

From **GOLD PRINT:**
- Cut 5, 2-1/2 x 42-inch strips. From the strips cut: 80, 2-1/2-inch center squares

From *each* of the **18 ASSORTED DARK PRINTS:**
- Cut 5, 1-1/2 x 42-inch strips

From *each* of the **7 ASSORTED BEIGE PRINTS:**
- Cut 12, 1-1/2 x 42-inch strips

Piecing

Note: *Vary the position of the* **BEIGE PRINT** *fabrics from block to block to get a scrappy look. The same is true of the* **DARK PRINT** *fabrics. Follow Steps 1 through 5 to piece each of the 80 Log Cabin blocks.*

Step 1 Sew a 1-1/2-inch wide **BEIGE PRINT** strip to a 2-1/2-inch **GOLD** square. Press the seam allowance toward the strip. Trim the strip even with the edges of the center square creating a 2-piece unit.

Trim

Make 80

Step 2   Turn the unit a quarter turn to the left and stitch a *different* 1-1/2-inch wide **BEIGE PRINT** strip to the unit; press and trim.

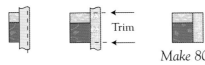

Make 80

Step 3   Turn the unit a quarter turn to the left and stitch a 1-1/2-inch wide **DARK PRINT** strip to the unit; press and trim.

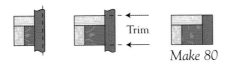

Make 80

Step 4   Turn the unit a quarter turn to the left and stitch a *different* 1-1/2-inch wide **DARK PRINT** strip to the unit; press and trim.

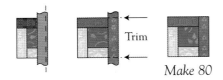

Make 80

Step 5   Referring to the block diagram, continue adding the 1-1/2-inch wide strips, alternating the **BEIGE PRINT** and **DARK PRINT** strips to complete the Log Cabin block. Press and trim each strip before adding the next. Each Log Cabin block should measure 8-1/2-inches square when complete. Adjust the seam allowances if needed.

Make 80

Quilt Center

Quilt Center Assembly

Step 1   Referring to the quilt diagram for block placement, lay out the Log Cabin blocks in 10 rows of 8 blocks each.

Step 2   Sew the blocks together in each row. Press the seam allowances in alternating directions by rows so the seams will fit snugly together with less bulk.

Step 3   Pin the rows together at the block intersections and sew the rows together; press.

Putting It All Together

Cut the 4-3/4 yard length of backing fabric in half crosswise to make 2, 2-3/8 yard lengths. Refer to **Finishing the Quilt** on page 128 for complete instructions.

Binding

Cutting

From **BLACK PRINT:**
- Cut 8, 2-3/4 x 42-inch strips

Sew the binding to the quilt using a 3/8-inch seam allowance. This measurement will produce a 1/2-inch wide finished double binding. Refer to **Binding** and **Diagonal Piecing** on page 128 for complete instructions.

Harvest Log Cabin Quilt
64 x 80-inches

Harvest Bounty

Small squash and petite pumpkins are golden accents for a handsome harvest table top arrangement.

18-inches square

Fabrics & Supplies

1-3/8 yards   **BEIGE PRINT** for appliqué foundation square, pillow top lining, and pillow back

10-inch square   **ORANGE PRINT #1** for pumpkin appliqués (outer sections)

9-inch square   **ORANGE PRINT #2** for pumpkin appliqués (side/top sections)

3 x 8-inch piece   **ORANGE PRINT #3** for pumpkin appliqué (center section)

4-inch square   **GREEN PRINT** for stem appliqué

1/2 yard   **GREEN DIAGONAL PRINT** for ruffle

quilt batting, at least 22-inches square

18-inch square pillow form

freezer paper for appliqués

pearl cotton for decorative stitches: black

template material

*NOTE: read **Getting Started**, page 123, before beginning this project.*

Pillow Top
Freezer Paper Appliqué Method

Note: *With this method of hand appliqué, the freezer paper forms a base around which the appliqués are shaped.*

Cutting

From **BEIGE PRINT:**
- Cut 1, 22-inch pillow lining square. Set this square aside to be used in the **PUTTING IT ALL TOGETHER** section.
- Cut 1, 18-1/2-inch appliqué foundation square

Prepare the Appliqués

Step 1   Make templates using the shapes on pages 37, 38 and 39. Trace the shapes on the paper side of the freezer paper the number of times indicated on each pattern. Cut out the shapes on the traced lines.

Step 2   With a hot, dry iron, press the coated side of each freezer paper shape onto the wrong side of the fabric chosen for the appliqués. Allow at least 1/2-inch between each shape for seam allowances.

Step 3   Cut out each shape a scant 1/4-inch beyond the edge of the freezer paper pattern.

Step 4   Referring to the pillow assembly diagram, position the pumpkin and stem shapes on the 18-1/2-inch **BEIGE** appliqué foundation square, overlapping them as shown; pin in place. Hand appliqué the shapes in place with matching thread.

Step 5 The tendrils were embroidered using pearl cotton and the stem stitch.

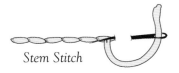
Stem Stitch

Putting It All Together

Step 1 Layer the 22-inch **BEIGE** lining square (cut previously), batting, and appliquéd pillow top. Hand baste the layers together and quilt as desired. When quilting is complete, trim the excess lining and batting even with the pillow top.

Step 2 Hand baste the edges together. This will prevent the edge of the pillow top from rippling when it is sewn to the backing.

Ruffle

Cutting

From **GREEN DIAGONAL PRINT:**
• Cut 4, 3-1/2 x 42-inch strips for the ruffle

Attaching the Ruffle

Step 1 Diagonally piece the 3-1/2-inch wide **GREEN DIAGONAL PRINT** strips together to make a continuos ruffle strip, referring to **Diagonal Piecing** instructions on page 128.

Step 2 Fold the strip in half lengthwise, wrong sides together; press. Divide the ruffle strip into 4 equal segments; mark the quarter points with safety pins.

Step 3 To gather the ruffle, position a heavyweight thread a scant 1/4-inch from the raw edges of the folded ruffle strip. You will need a length of thread 180-inches long. Secure 1 end of the thread by stitching across it. Zigzag stitch over the thread all the way around the ruffle strip, taking care not to sew through it.

secure
zigzag

Step 4 Divide the edges of the appliquéd pillow top into 4 equal segments; mark the quarter points with safety pins. With right sides together, raw edges aligned, and quarter points

matching, pin the prepared ruffle to the **BEIGE** pillow top. Pull up the gathering stitches until the ruffle fits the pillow top, taking care to allow extra fullness in the ruffle at each corner. Sew the ruffle in place using a scant 1/4-inch seam allowance.

Pillow Back

Cutting

From **BEIGE PRINT:**
• Cut 1, 24 x 42-inch strip. From the strip cut: 2, 18-1/2 x 24-inch pillow back rectangles

Assembling the Pillow Back

Step 1 With wrong sides together, fold each **BEIGE** pillow back rectangle in half crosswise to make 2, 12 x 18-1/2-inch double-thick pillow back pieces. Overlap the 2 folded edges so the pillow back measures 18-1/2-inches square. Pin the pieces together and machine baste around the entire piece to create a single pillow back, using a 1/4-inch seam allowance. The double thickness of the pillow back will make it more stable and give it a nice finishing touch.

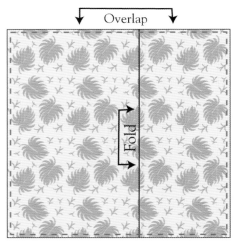
Overlap
Fold

Step 2 With right sides together, layer the pillow back and the pillow top; pin. The ruffle will be sandwiched between the 2 layers and turned in toward the center of the pillow at this time. Pin and stitch around the outside edges using a 3/8-inch seam allowance.

Step 3 Turn the pillow right side out and insert the pillow form through the back opening. Fluff up the ruffle.

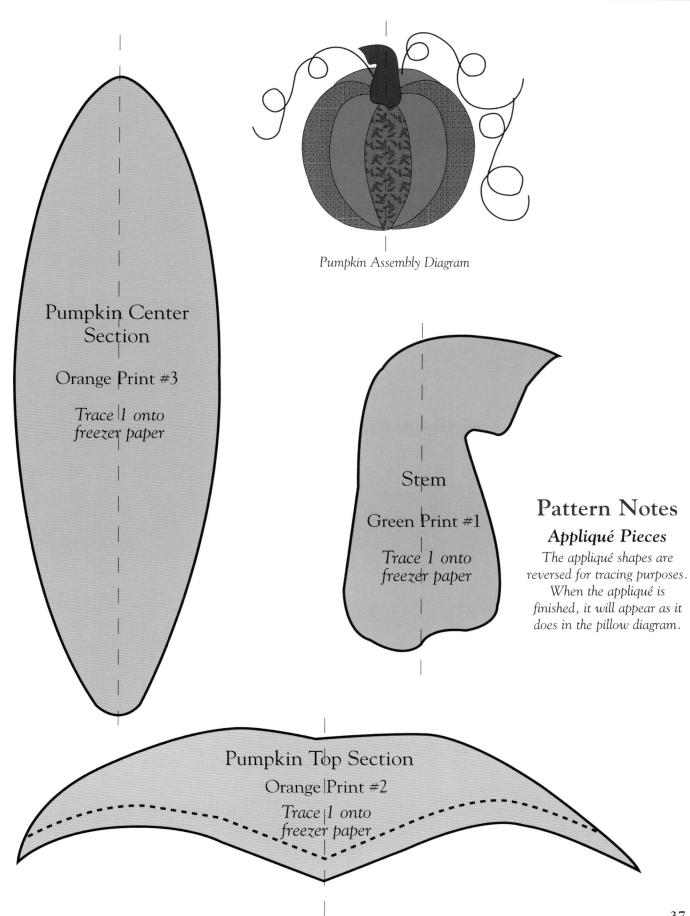

Pumpkin Center
Section

Orange Print #3

Trace 1 onto
freezer paper

Pumpkin Assembly Diagram

Stem

Green Print #1

Trace 1 onto
freezer paper

Pattern Notes
Appliqué Pieces
*The appliqué shapes are
reversed for tracing purposes.
When the appliqué is
finished, it will appear as it
does in the pillow diagram.*

Pumpkin Top Section

Orange Print #2

Trace 1 onto
freezer paper

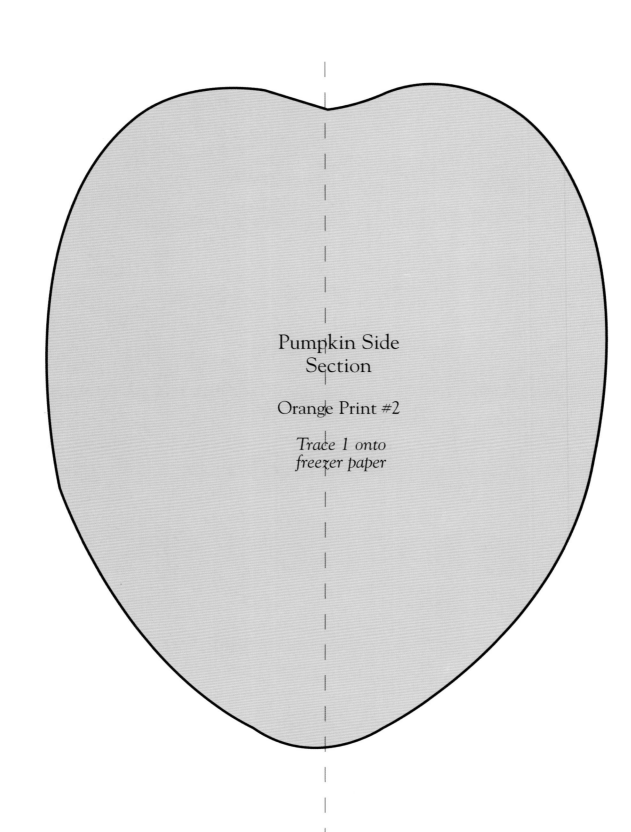

Pumpkin Side
Section

Orange Print #2

*Trace 1 onto
freezer paper*

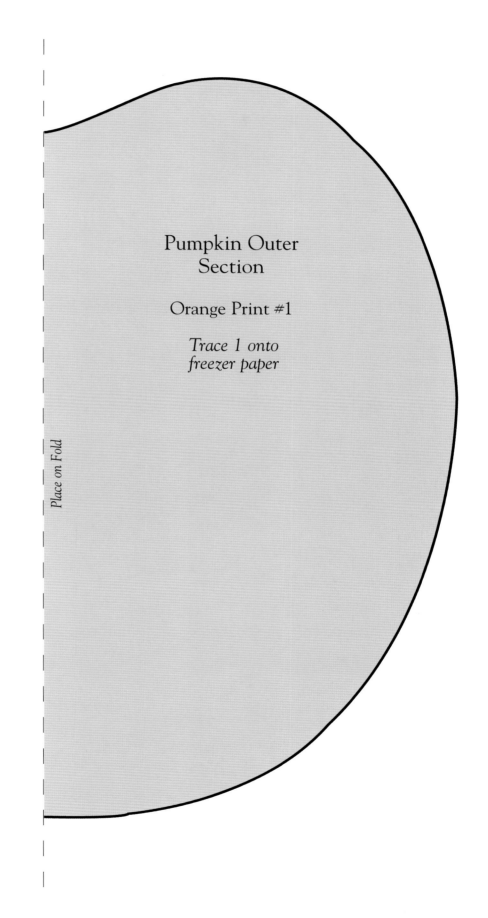

Pumpkin Outer
Section

Orange Print #1

*Trace 1 onto
freezer paper*

Place on Fold

Harvest Bounty Pillow
18-inches square

Add a splash of color to a gathering of dried garden findings with a trio of pumpkins for quick and casual autumn displays.

Fence Sitting

Decorating with pumpkins— as easy as one, two, three!

Table Runner

26 x 38-inches

Fabrics & Supplies

1/8 yard	**ORANGE FLORAL** for inner pumpkin units
5/8 yard	**ORANGE PUMPKIN PRINT** for outer pumpkin units and outer border
5/8 yard	**BLACK PRINT** for quilt center and dogtooth border
1/4 yard	**TAN PRINT** for picket fence
1/3 yard	**GREEN PRINT** for pumpkin stems and dogtooth border
1/4 yard	**ORANGE PRINT** for inner border
3/8 yard	**BLACK PRINT** for binding

1-1/4 yards for backing

quilt batting, at least 32 x 44-inches

*NOTE: read **Getting Started**, page 123, before beginning this project.*

Pumpkin Section

Cutting

From **ORANGE FLORAL**:
- Cut 1, 2-1/2 x 42-inch strip.
  From the strip cut:
  3, 2-1/2 x 6-1/2-inch rectangles

From **ORANGE PUMPKIN PRINT**:
- Cut 2, 2-1/2 x 42-inch strips.
  From the strips cut:
  6, 2-1/2 x 6-1/2-inch rectangles
  6, 1-1/2-inch squares

From **BLACK PRINT**:
- Cut 1, 3-1/2 x 42-inch strip.
  From the strip cut:
  2, 3-1/2 x 8-1/2-inch rectangles
  3, 2-1/2 x 3-1/2-inch rectangles
  3, 2-1/2-inch squares
- Cut 1, 1-1/2 x 42-inch strip. From the strip cut:
  15, 1-1/2-inch squares

From **GREEN PRINT**:
- Cut 1, 1-1/2 x 42-inch strip.
  From the strip cut:
  3, 1-1/2 x 2-1/2-inch rectangles
  12, 1-1/2-inch squares

Piecing

Step 1 With right sides together, position a 1-1/2-inch **GREEN** square on the upper left corner of a 2-1/2 x 6-1/2-inch **ORANGE FLORAL** rectangle. Draw a diagonal line on the square; stitch, trim, and press. Repeat this process at the adjacent corner of the rectangle. Repeat this process at the lower corners of the rectangle using 1-1/2-inch **ORANGE PUMPKIN PRINT** squares.

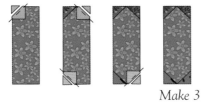

Make 3

Step 2 Sew 2-1/2 x 6-1/2-inch **ORANGE PUMPKIN PRINT** rectangles to both side edges of each Step 1 unit; press. Position 1-1/2-inch **BLACK** squares on the corners of the units. Draw diagonal lines on the squares; stitch, trim, and press. <u>At this point each pumpkin unit should measure 6-1/2-inches square.</u>

Make 3 pumpkin units

Step 3 To make the stem units, position a 1-1/2-inch **GREEN** square on the corner of a 2-1/2 x 3-1/2-inch **BLACK** rectangle. Draw a diagonal line on the square; stitch, trim, and press. Repeat this process at the adjacent corner of the rectangle.

Make 3

Step 4 With right sides together, position a 1-1/2-inch **BLACK** square on the top corner of a 1-1/2 x 3-1/2-inch **GREEN** rectangle. Draw a diagonal line on the square; stitch, trim, and press. Make 3 units. Sew a 2-1/2-inch **BLACK** square to the left edge of each unit; press.

Make 3

Step 5 Sew the Step 4 units to the left edge of each Step 3 unit; press. Make 3 stem units. Sew the stem units to the top edge of the Step 2 pumpkin units; press. <u>At this point each pumpkin block should measure 6-1/2 x 8-1/2-inches.</u>

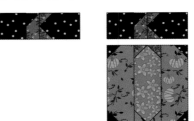

Make 3

Step 6 Referring to the quilt diagram sew together the 3 pumpkin blocks and the 1-1/2 x 8-1/2-inch **BLACK** rectangles; press. Sew the 3-1/2 x 8-1/2-inch **BLACK** rectangles to both side edges of the unit; press. <u>At this point the quilt center should measure 8-1/2 x 26-1/2-inches.</u>

Picket Fence Section

Cutting

From **TAN PRINT**:
- Cut 2, 2-1/2 x 42-inch strips. From the strips cut:
  9, 2-1/2 x 6-1/2-inch rectangles
  1, 1-1/2 x 16-inch strip

From **BLACK PRINT**:
- Cut 1, 3-1/2 x 42-inch strip. From the strip cut:
  1, 3-1/2 x 16-inch strip
  1, 2-1/2 x 16-inch strip
- Cut 1, 1-1/2 x 42-inch strip. From the strip cut:
  18, 1-1/2-inch squares

Piecing

Step 1 Aligning long edges, sew together the 2-1/2 x 16-inch **BLACK** strip, the 3-1/2 x 16-inch **BLACK** strip, and the 1-1/2 x 16-inch **TAN** strip; press. Cut the strip set into segments.

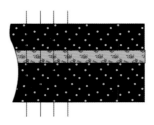

Crosscut 8, 1-1/2-inch wide segments

44

Step 2 With right sides together, position a 1-1/2-inch **BLACK** square on the upper left corner of a 2-1/2 x 6-1/2-inch **TAN** rectangle. Draw a diagonal line on the square; stitch, trim, and press. Repeat this process at the adjacent corner of the rectangle.

Make 9 picket fence units

Step 3 Sew together the Step 2 picket fence units and the Step 1 segments; press. <u>At this point the picket fence section should measure 6-1/2 x 26-1/2-inches.</u>

Step 4 Referring to the quilt diagram, sew together the picket fence section and the pumpkin section. <u>At this point the quilt center should measure 14-1/2 x 26-1/2-inches.</u>

Borders

*Note: The yardage given allows for the border strips to be cut on the crosswise grain. Read through **Border** instructions on pages 127–128 for general instructions on adding borders.*

Cutting

From **ORANGE PRINT:**
• Cut 3, 1-1/2 x 42-inch inner border strips

From **BLACK PRINT:**
• Cut 3, 2-1/2 x 42-inch strips. From the strips cut: 44, 2-1/2-inch squares

From **GREEN PRINT:**
• Cut 3, 2-1/2 x 42-inch strips. From the strips cut: 22, 2-1/2 x 4-1/2-inch rectangles 4, 2-1/2-inch squares

From **ORANGE PUMPKIN PRINT:**
• Cut 4, 3-1/2 x 42-inch outer border strips

Assembling and Attaching the Borders

Step 1 Attach the 1-1/2-inch wide **ORANGE PRINT** inner border strips.

Step 2 With right sides together, position a 2-1/2-inch **BLACK** square on the corner of a 2-1/2 x 4-1/2-inch **GREEN** rectangle. Draw a diagonal line on the square; stitch, trim, and press. Repeat this process at the opposite corner of the rectangle.

Make 22 dogtooth units

Step 3 For the top/bottom dogtooth borders, sew together 7 of the dogtooth units; press. Sew the dogtooth borders to the quilt center; press

Step 4 For the side dogtooth borders, sew together 4 of the dogtooth units; press. Sew the 2-1/2-inch **GREEN** squares to both ends of the border strips; press. Sew the dogtooth borders to the quilt center; press.

Step 5 Attach the 3-1/2-inch wide **ORANGE PUMPKIN PRINT** outer border strips.

Putting It All Together

Trim the backing and batting so they are 6-inches larger than the quilt top. Refer to **Finishing the Quilt** on page 128 for complete instructions.

Binding

From **BLACK PRINT:**
• Cut 4, 2-3/4 x 42-inch binding strips

Sew the binding to the quilt using a 3/8-inch seam allowance. This measurement will produce a 1/2-inch wide finished double binding. Refer to **Binding** and **Diagonal Piecing** on page 128 for complete instructions.

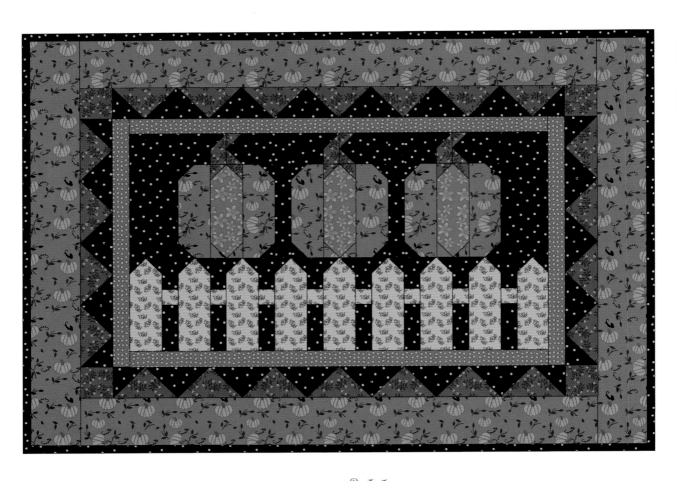

Fence Sitting Table Runner
26 x 38-inches

Pumpkins and gourds are members of the squash family with such amusing names as Little Boo, Jack Be Little, and Munchkin.

Autumn Night

For sparkling warmth on chilly autumn evenings, fill an old copper tub with floating novelty candles.

Wall Quilt

58-inches square

Fabrics & Supplies

1/2 yard	**GOLD PRINT** for stars and inner border
1-1/4 yards	**BLACK PRINT** for star blocks and outer border
3/8 yard	**BEIGE PRINT** for nine-patch blocks and pumpkin block
1/4 yard	**GREEN PRINT #1** for nine-patch blocks and stem
1/4 yard	**TAN/PURPLE FLORAL** for quilt center blocks
1/3 yard	**ORANGE PRINT** for quilt center blocks and pumpkin block
3/8 yard	**RUST PRINT** for pumpkin block and corner squares
1-1/8 yards	**GREEN PRINT #2** for fence background, corner squares, and vine appliqué
5/8 yard	**CREAM PRINT** for fence border
5/8 yard	**GOLD PRINT** for binding

3-3/4 yards for backing

quilt batting, at least 64-inches square

NOTE: *read* **Getting Started**, *page 123, before beginning this project.*

Star Blocks

Makes 5 blocks
Cutting

From **GOLD PRINT**:
- Cut 2, 2-1/2 x 42-inch strips.
  From the strips cut:
  5, 2-1/2 x 6-1/2-inch rectangles
  10, 2-1/2-inch squares

From **BLACK PRINT**:
- Cut 3, 2-1/2 x 42-inch strips.
  From the strips cut:
  10, 2-1/2 x 4-1/2-inch rectangles
  20, 2-1/2-inch squares

Piecing

Step 1 With right sides together, position 2-1/2-inch **BLACK** squares on both corners of a 2-1/2 x 6-1/2-inch **GOLD** rectangle. Draw a diagonal line on the squares and stitch on the lines. Trim the seam allowances to 1/4-inch; press.

Make 5

Step 2 Position a 2-1/2-inch **GOLD** square on the right corner of a 2-1/2 x 4-1/2-inch **BLACK** rectangle. Draw a diagonal line on the square; stitch, trim, and press. Sew a 2-1/2-inch **BLACK** square to the right edge of the unit; press.

Make 10

Step 3 Sew Step 2 units to the top/bottom edges of a Step 1 unit; press. <u>At this point each star block should measure 6-1/2-inches square.</u>

Make 5

Pumpkin Block

Cutting

From **BEIGE PRINT**:
• Cut 1, 4-1/2 x 42-inch strip. From the strip cut:
 2, 4-1/2 x 5-1/2-inch rectangles
 5, 2-1/2-inch squares

From **GREEN PRINT #1**:
• Cut 1, 2-1/2 x 4-1/2-inch rectangle
• Cut 2, 1-1/2-inch squares

From **ORANGE PRINT**:
• Cut 1, 2-1/2 x 42-inch strip. From the strip cut:
 2, 2-1/2 x 14-1/2-inch rectangles

From **RUST PRINT**:
• Cut 1, 4-1/2 x 42-inch strip. From the strip cut:
 2, 4-1/2 x 14-1/2-inch rectangles
 2, 2-1/2-inch squares

Piecing

Step 1 Position a 2-1/2-inch **BEIGE** square on the corner of a 2-1/2 x 4-1/2-inch **GREEN #1** rectangle. Draw a diagonal line on the square; stitch, trim, and press. Sew 4-1/2 x 5-1/2-inch **BEIGE** rectangles to both side edges of the stem unit; press. <u>At this point the stem section should measure 4-1/2 x 12-1/2-inches.</u>

Make 1

Step 2 Position 2-1/2-inch **BEIGE** squares on the upper corners of a 4-1/2 x 14-1/2-inch **RUST** rectangle. Draw a diagonal line on the squares; stitch, trim, and press.

Make 2

Step 3 Position a 2-1/2-inch **RUST** square on the left corner of a 2-1/2 x 14-1/2-inch **ORANGE** rectangle. Draw a diagonal line on the square; stitch, trim, and press. Position a 1-1/2-inch **GREEN #1** square on the lower right corner of this unit. Draw a diagonal line on the square; stitch, trim, and press.

Make 1

Step 4 Position a 2-1/2-inch **RUST** square on the right corner of a 2-1/2 x 14-1/2-inch **ORANGE** rectangle. Draw a diagonal line on the square; stitch, trim, and press. Position a 1-1/2-inch **GREEN #1** square on the lower left corner of this unit. Draw a diagonal line on the square; stitch, trim, and press.

Make 1

Step 5 Referring to the block diagram for placement, sew the Step 3 and Step 4 units together; press. Sew the Step 2 units to both side edges of this unit; press. Sew the Step 1 stem section to the top edge of this section; press. <u>At this point the pumpkin block should measure 12-1/2 x 18-1/2-inches.</u>

Make 1

Nine-Patch Blocks

Makes 5 blocks

Cutting

From **BEIGE PRINT**:
• Cut 2, 2-1/2 x 42-inch strips
• Cut 1, 2-1/2 x 20-inch strip

From **GREEN PRINT #1**:
• Cut 1, 2-1/2 x 42-inch strip
• Cut 2, 2-1/2 x 20-inch strips

Piecing

Step 1 Aligning long edges, sew a 2-1/2 x 42-inch **BEIGE** strip to both side edges of a 2-1/2 x 42-inch **GREEN #1** strip. Press, referring to **Hints and Helps for Pressing Strip Sets** on page 127. Cut the strip set into segments.

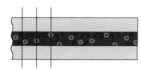

Crosscut 10, 2-1/2-inch wide segments

Step 2 Aligning long edges, sew a 2-1/2 x 20-inch **GREEN #1** strip to both side edges of a 2-1/2 x 20-inch **BEIGE** strip; press. Cut the strip set into segments.

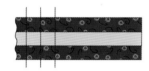

Crosscut 5, 2-1/2-inch wide segments

Step 3 Sew Step 1 units to both side edges of a Step 2 unit; press. At this point each nine-patch block should measure 6-1/2-inches square.

Make 5

Quilt Center and Inner Border

Cutting

From **TAN/PURPLE FLORAL**:
- Cut 1, 6-1/2 x 42-inch strip. From the strip cut: 2, 6-1/2 x 12-1/2-inch rectangles 2, 6-1/2-inch squares

From **ORANGE PRINT**:
- Cut 1, 6-1/2 x 42-inch strip. From the strip cut: 3, 6-1/2-inch squares

From **GREEN PRINT #2**:
- Cut 1, 1-3/8 x 27-inch **bias** strip for left vine
- Cut 1, 1-3/8 x 37-inch **bias** strip for center vine
- Cut 1, 1-3/8 x 33-inch **bias** strip for right vine

From **GOLD PRINT**:
- Cut 4, 2-1/2 x 42-inch inner border strips

Quilt Center Assembly

Step 1 Referring to the quilt assembly diagram, sew the nine-patch blocks, star blocks, **TAN/PURPLE FLORAL** squares and rectangles, **ORANGE** squares, and pumpkin block together in horizontal rows. Press the seam allowances in alternating directions by rows so the seams will fit snugly together with less bulk.

Step 2 Sew the rows together to make the quilt center; press. At this point the quilt center should measure 30-1/2-inches square.

Step 3 Attach the 2-1/2-inch wide **GOLD** inner border strips. Read through **Border** instructions on pages 127–128 for general instructions on adding borders.

Quilt Assembly Diagram

Prepare the Vine Appliqués

Fold each 1-3/8-inch wide **GREEN #2** strip in half lengthwise with wrong sides together; press. To keep the raw edges aligned, stitch a scant 1/4-inch away from the raw edges. Fold each strip in half again so the raw edges are hidden by the first folded edge; press. Referring to the quilt diagram; pin the vines in place. Notice that the vines start in the seam between the pumpkin and the stem. Take a few stitches out of the seam, insert the ends of the vines; stitch the opening closed. With matching thread, appliqué the vines in place.

51

Fence Border and Outer Border

Note: *The yardage given allows for the border strips to be cut on the crosswise grain. Diagonally piece the strips as needed, referring to* **Diagonal Piecing** *on page 128 for complete instructions. Read through* **Border** *instructions on pages 127-128 for general instructions on adding borders.*

Cutting

From GREEN PRINT #2:
- Cut 1, 6-1/2 x 42-inch strip. From the strip cut: 4, 6-1/2-inch corner squares
- Cut 3, 2-1/2 x 42-inch strips. From the strips cut: 36, 2-1/2-inch squares
- Cut 4 more 2-1/2 x 42-inch strips

From CREAM PRINT:
- Cut 6, 2-1/2 x 42-inch strips. From the strips cut: 36, 2-1/2 x 6-1/2-inch rectangles
- Cut 2 more 2-1/2 x 42-inch strips

From BLACK PRINT:
- Cut 5, 6-1/2 x 42-inch outer border strips

From RUST PRINT:
- Cut 1, 6-1/2 x 42-inch strip. From the strip cut: 4, 6-1/2-inch corner squares

Piecing and Attaching the Borders

Step 1 Position a 2-1/2-inch **GREEN #2** square on the upper corner of a 2-1/2 x 6-1/2-inch **CREAM** rectangle. Draw a diagonal line on the square; stitch, trim, and press.

 *Make 36*

Step 2 Aligning long edges, sew a 2-1/2 x 42-inch **GREEN #2** strip to both side edges of a 2-1/2 x 42-inch **CREAM** strip; press. Make 2 strip sets. Cut the strip sets into segments.

Crosscut 32, 2-1/2-inch wide segments

Step 3 Referring to the diagram for placement, sew together 9 of the Step 1 units and 8 of the Step 2 segments; press. Make 4 fence borders. <u>At this point each fence border should measure 6-1/2 x 34-1/2-inches.</u>

Make 4

Step 4 Referring to the quilt diagram, sew fence borders to the top/bottom edges of the quilt center; press. Sew 6-1/2-inch **GREEN #2** corner squares to both ends of the remaining fence borders; press. Sew the borders to the side edges of the quilt center; press.

Step 5 Attach the 6-1/2-inch wide **BLACK** top/bottom outer border strips.

Step 6 For the side outer borders, measure the quilt from top to bottom, including the seam allowances but not the borders just added. Cut the 6-1/2-inch wide **BLACK** side outer border strips to this length. Sew 6-1/2-inch **RUST** corner squares to both ends of the borders strips; press. Sew the border strips to the side edges of the quilt center.

Putting It All Together

Cut the 3-3/4 yard length of backing fabric in half crosswise to make 2, 1-7/8 yard lengths. Refer to **Finishing the Quilt** on page 128 for complete instructions.

Binding

Cutting

From GOLD PRINT:
- Cut 7, 2-3/4 x 42-inch strips

Sew the binding to the quilt using a 3/8-inch seam allowance. This measurement will produce a 1/2-inch wide finished double binding. Refer to **Binding** and **Diagonal Piecing** on page 128 for complete instructions.

Autumn Night Wall Quilt

58-inches square

The Great Pumpkin

A white pumpkin adds interest and contrast to the earthy brown hues of autumn.

Wall Quilt

25-inches square
Fabrics & Supplies

1/3 yard	**DARK GREEN PRINT** for checkerboard border and large leaf appliqué
3/8 yard	**BEIGE PRINT** for appliqué foundation and checkerboard border
2/3 yard	**GOLD FLORAL** for outer border
4-inch square	**BROWN PRINT #1** for stem appliqué
1/8 yard	**ORANGE PRINT** for pumpkin appliqués A and C
4 x 16-inch piece	**GOLD PRINT** for pumpkin appliqué B
3/8 yard	**GREEN PRINT #1** for vine appliqués
1/8 yard	**RED PRINT #1** for large leaf appliqués
1/8 yard	**GREEN PRINT #2** for small pieced leaf appliqués
1/8 yard	**RED PRINT #2** for small pieced leaf appliqués
1/8 yard	**BROWN PRINT #2** for small leaf appliqués
1/3 yard	**DARK GREEN PRINT** for binding

7/8 yard for backing

quilt batting, at least 31-inches square

paper-backed fusible web for appliqué

machine embroidery thread or pearl cotton for decorative stitches: black

tear-away fabric stabilizer (optional)

*NOTE: read **Getting Started**, page 123, before beginning this project.*

Center Square and Checkerboard Border

Cutting

From **DARK GREEN PRINT:**
• Cut 3, 1-1/2 x 42-inch strips

From **BEIGE PRINT**:
• Cut 1, 7-1/2-inch square
• Cut 3, 1-1/2 x 42-inch strips

Note: *The checkerboard is made up of strip sets. To press strip sets, refer to **Hints and Helps for Pressing Strip Sets** on page 127.*

Piecing

Step 1   Aligning long edges, sew a 1-1/2 x 42-inch **DARK GREEN** strip to both side edges of a 1-1/2 x 42-inch **BEIGE** strip; press. Cut the strip set into segments.

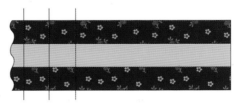

Crosscut 20, 1-1/2-inch wide segments

Step 2 Aligning long edges, sew a 1-1/2 x 42-inch **BEIGE** strip to both side edges of a 1-1/2 x 42-inch **DARK GREEN** strip; press. Cut the strip set into segments.

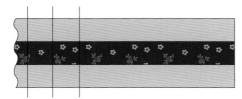

Crosscut 20, 1-1/2-inch wide segments

Step 3 To make the top checkerboard border, sew 3 of the Step 1 segments and 4 of the Step 2 segments together; press. Repeat for the bottom border. <u>At this point each checkerboard border should measure 3-1/2 x 7-1/2-inches.</u> Sew the checkerboard borders to the top/bottom edges of the 7-1/2-inch **BEIGE** square; press.

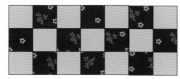

Make 2

Step 4 To make the side checkerboard borders, sew 7 of the Step 1 segments and 6 of the Step 2 segments together; press. Make 2 checkerboard borders. <u>At this point each checkerboard border should measure 3-1/2 x 13-1/2-inches.</u> Sew the checkerboard borders to the side edges of the unit; press.

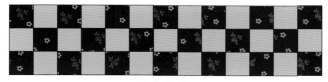

Make 2

Outer Border

Note: *The yardage given allows for the border strips to be cut on the crosswise grain. Diagonally piece the strips as needed, referring to* **Diagonal Piecing** *instructions on page 128. Read through* **Border** *instructions on pages 127–128 for general instructions on adding borders.*

Cutting

From **GOLD FLORAL:**
• Cut 3, 6-1/2 x 42-inch outer border strips

Attaching the Border

Attach the 6-1/2-inch wide **GOLD FLORAL** outer border strips.

Vine Appliqué

Cutting

From **GREEN PRINT #1:**
• Cut enough 1-3/4-inch wide **bias** strips to make a 45-inch long strip.

Attaching the Vines

Step 1 Diagonally piece the **GREEN #1 bias** strips together, referring to **Diagonal Piecing** instructions on page 128.

Step 2 Fold the **GREEN #1** strip in half lengthwise with wrong sides together; press. Stitch a scant 1/4-inch from the raw edges to keep them aligned. Fold the strip in half lengthwise so the raw edges are hidden by the first folded edge; press. <u>At this point the vine strip should measure about 1/2-inch wide.</u>

Cutting

From Vine Strip:
• Cut 1, 25-inch long strip
• Cut 1, 10-inch long strip
• Cut 2, 5-inch long strips

Step 3 Referring to the quilt diagram, position the vine strips on the pieced quilt top. Tuck the ends of the 5-inch long vines under the longer vines; pin. Hand appliqué the vines in place with matching thread.

Pumpkin and Leaf Appliqué

Fusible Web Technique

Prepare the Appliqués

Step 1 Position the fusible web (paper side up) over the appliqué shapes. With a pencil, trace the shapes the number of times as indicated on each pattern, leaving a small margin between each shape. Cut the shapes apart.

Cutting

From **RED PRINT #1:**
- Cut 1, 4-1/2 x 42-inch strip for pieced large leaf

From **DARK GREEN PRINT:**
- Cut 1, 4-1/2 x 42-inch strip for pieced large leaf

From **RED PRINT #2:**
- Cut 1, 3 x 18-inch strip for pieced small leaf

From **GREEN PRINT #2:**
- Cut 1, 3 x 18-inch strip for pieced small leaf

Step 2 Aligning long edges, sew the 4-1/2 x 42-inch **RED #1** and **DARK GREEN** strips together; press. Center the large leaf fusible web shape on the wrong side of the **RED #1/DARK GREEN** unit having the leaf centered on the seam. Fuse 3 large leaves to the **RED #1/DARK GREEN** unit having the **RED #1** fabric on the right hand side and fuse 1 large leaf fusible web shape to the unit having the **RED #1** fabric on the left hand side.

Step 3 Aligning long edges, sew the 3 x 18-inch **RED #2** and **GREEN #2** strips together; press. Center the small leaf fusible web shape on the wrong side of the **RED #2/GREEN #2** unit having the leaf centered on the seam line. Fuse 4 small leaves to the **RED #2/GREEN #2** unit having the **RED #2** fabric on the right hand side.

Step 4 Following the manufacturer's instructions, fuse the remaining 3 small leaf shapes to the wrong side of the **BROWN #2** fabric. Let the fabric cool and cut along the traced line of each shape. Peel away the paper backing from the fusible web.

Step 5 Referring to the quilt diagram, position the appliqué shapes on the quilt, layering them as needed; fuse in place. We suggest pinning a rectangle of tear-away stabilizer to the backside of the fabric to be appliquéd on so that it will lay flat when the appliqué is complete. We use the extra-lightweight Easy Tear™ sheets as a stabilizer. When the appliqué is complete, tear away the stabilizer.

Step 6 Our project was machine blanket stitched with black machine embroidery thread. Outline/stem stitch along the seam line of the pieced leaves with black machine embroidery thread. If you like you could use pearl cotton to hand blanket stitch the shapes in place.

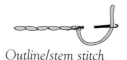

Outline/stem stitch

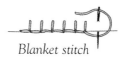

Blanket stitch

Note: *To prevent the hand blanket stitches from "rolling off" the edges of the appliqué shapes, take an extra backstitch in the same place as you made the blanket stitch, going around outer curves, corners, and points. For straight edges, taking a backstitch every inch is enough.*

Putting It All Together

Trim the batting and backing so they are 6-inches larger than the quilt top. Refer to **Finishing the Quilt** on page 128 for complete instructions.

Binding

Cutting

From **DARK GREEN PRINT:**
- Cut 3, 2-3/4 x 42-inch strips

Sew the binding to the quilt using a 3/8-inch seam allowance. This measurement will produce a 1/2-inch wide finished double binding. Refer to **Binding** and **Diagonal Piecing** page 128 for complete instructions.

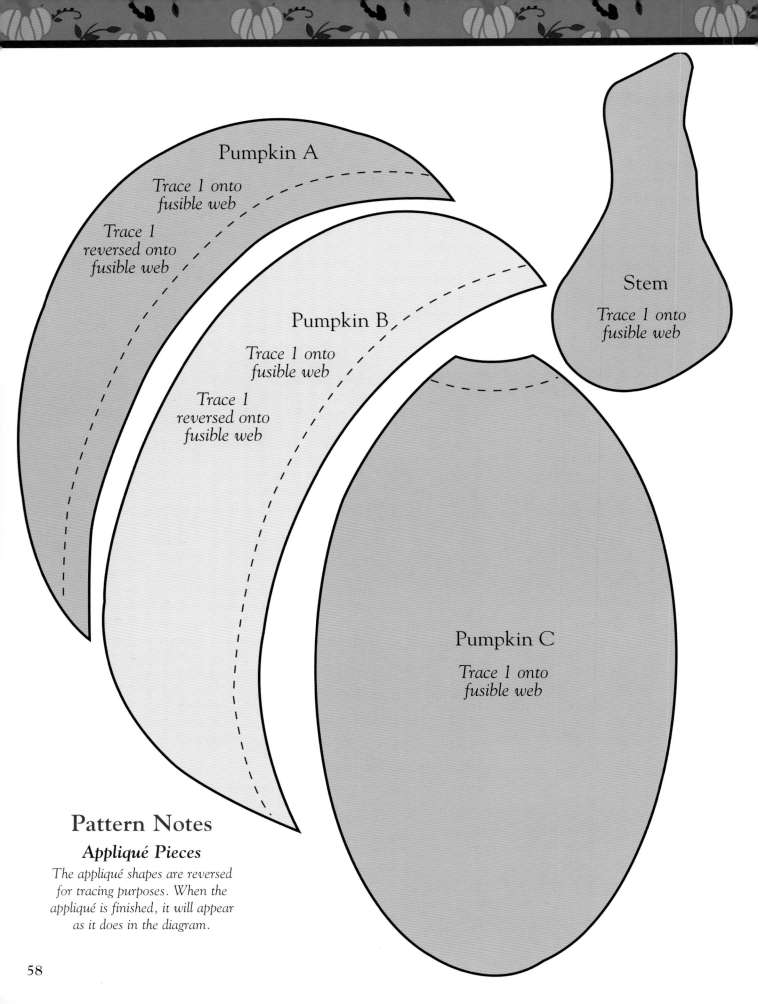

Pumpkin A

*Trace 1 onto
fusible web*

*Trace 1
reversed onto
fusible web*

Pumpkin B

*Trace 1 onto
fusible web*

*Trace 1
reversed onto
fusible web*

Stem

*Trace 1 onto
fusible web*

Pumpkin C

*Trace 1 onto
fusible web*

Pattern Notes

Appliqué Pieces

*The appliqué shapes are reversed
for tracing purposes. When the
appliqué is finished, it will appear
as it does in the diagram.*

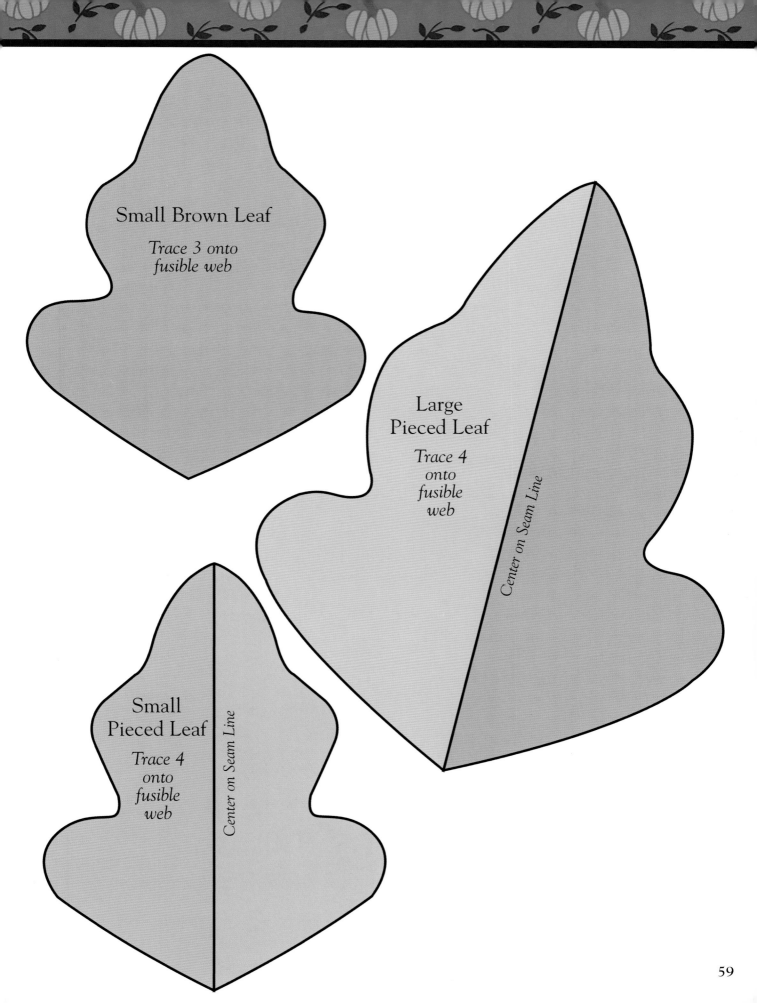

Small Brown Leaf

Trace 3 onto fusible web

Large Pieced Leaf

Trace 4 onto fusible web

Center on Seam Line

Small Pieced Leaf

Trace 4 onto fusible web

Center on Seam Line

The Great Pumpkin Wall Quilt
25-inches square

Turn your home into Halloween
headquarters with the many faces of the season!

Rick Rack Pumpkins

Display grinning gourd-pumpkin jack-o-lanterns on a trellis of Morning Glory vines and leaves.

Sampler

21-1/2-inches square

Fabrics & Supplies

4-1/2 x 25-inch piece	**ORANGE PRINT** for pumpkin appliqués
1/2 yard	**ORANGE PUMPKIN PRINT** for pumpkin appliqués and outer border
4-inch square	**GREEN PRINT** for pumpkin stem appliqués
3/8 yard	**TAN PRINT** for appliqué foundation squares
1/8 yard	**BLACK PRINT** for inner border
1/3 yard	**BLACK PRINT** for binding

3/4 yard for backing

quilt batting, at least 28-inches square

paper-backed fusible web for appliqué

pearl cotton or embroidery floss for decorative stitches: black

1/4-inch wide rick rack: black

tear-away fabric stabilizer (optional)

NOTE: read **Getting Started**, page 123, before beginning this project.

Pumpkin Blocks

Cutting

From **TAN PRINT**:
- Cut 9, 5-inch appliqué foundation squares

Prepare the Appliqués

Step 1 Position the fusible web, paper side up, over the appliqué shapes on page 64. Trace the shapes onto fusible web, leaving a small margin between each shape. Cut the shapes apart.

Step 2 Following the manufacturer's instructions, fuse the shapes to the wrong side of the fabric chosen for the appliqués. Let fabric cool and cut along the traced line.

Step 3 Referring to the block diagram, position the appliqué shapes on the 5-inch **TAN** appliqué foundation squares; fuse in place. Machine or hand appliqué the shapes in place using the blanket stitch.

block diagram

blanket stitch

Note: *If machine appliquéing, we suggest pinning a square of tear-away stabilizer to the backside of the appliqué foundation blocks so that they will lay flat when the appliqué is complete. We use the extra-lightweight Easy Tear™ sheets as a stabilizer. When the appliqué is complete, tear away the stabilizer.*

Step 4 The pumpkin sections were stitched using the running stitch.

running stitch

Quilt Center

Step 1 Sew the appliquéd blocks together in 3 rows of 3 blocks each. Press the seam allowances open to make it easier to attach the rick rack trim. Sew the rows together, pressing the seam allowances open.

Step 2 Position the black rick rack trim on the vertical seam lines and stitch in place. Position the rick rack trim on the horizontal seam lines; stitch in place and press. <u>At this point the quilt center should measure 14-inches square.</u>

Borders

Note: *The yardage given allows for the border strips to be cut on the crosswise grain. Read through* **Border** *instructions on pages 127–128 for general instructions on adding borders.*

Cutting

From **BLACK PRINT:**
• Cut 2, 1-1/2 x 42-inch inner border strips

From **ORANGE PUMPKIN PRINT:**
• Cut 3, 3-1/2 x 42-inch outer border strips

Attaching the Borders

Step 1 Attach the 1-1/2-inch wide **BLACK** inner border strips.

Step 2 Attach the 3-1/2-inch wide **ORANGE PUMPKIN PRINT** outer border strips.

Putting It All Together

Trim the backing and batting so they are approximately 6-inches larger than the quilt top. Refer to **Finishing the Quilt** on page 128 for complete instructions.

Binding

Cutting

From **BLACK PRINT:**
• Cut 3, 2-3/4 x 42-inch binding strips

Sew the binding to the quilt using a 3/8-inch seam allowance. This measurement will produce a 1/2-inch wide finished double binding. Refer to **Binding** and **Diagonal Piecing** on page 128 for complete instructions.

Stem
(Green Print)

Trace 9 onto fusible web

Pumpkin
(5 Orange Print and 4 Orange Pumpkin Print)

Trace 9 onto fusible web

Pattern Notes

Appliqué Pieces

The appliqué shapes are reversed for tracing purposes. When the appliqué is finished, it will appear as it does in the quilt diagram.

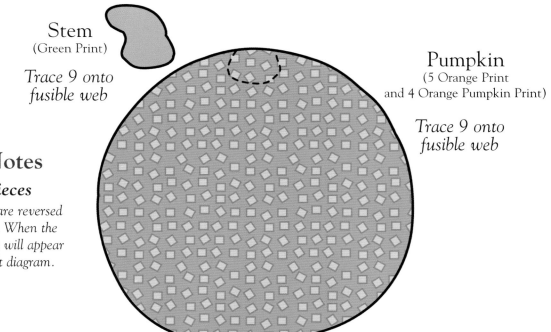

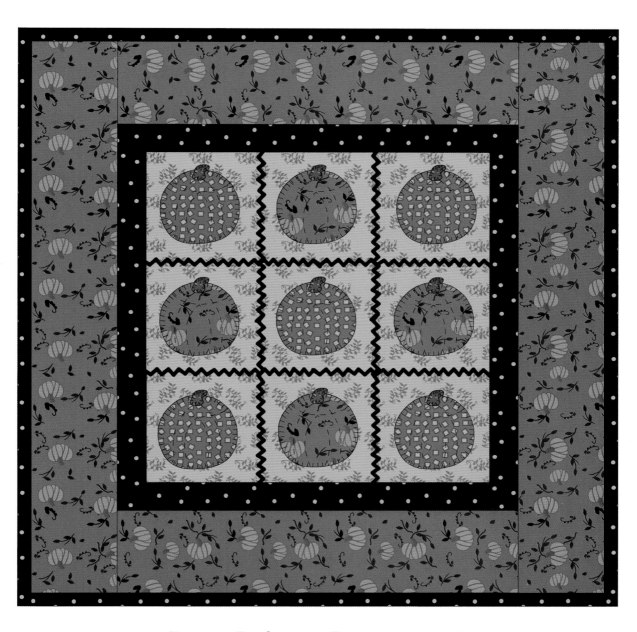

Rick Rack Pumpkins Sampler
21-1/2-inches square

Pumpkin Blossom

A blend of blossoms, leaves and a pumpkin offer an assortment of autumn's finest appliqué.

Wall Quilt

52-inches square

Fabrics & Supplies

5/8 yard	**BEIGE FLORAL** for appliqué foundation square and pieced inner border
1-1/8 yards	**MEDIUM GREEN PRINT** for pieced inner border, 2 middle borders, and dogtooth border
3/8 yard	**BLACK PRINT #1** for middle border
1/2 yard	**ORANGE FLORAL** for middle border and pumpkin section appliqués
1-1/4 yards	**BLACK PRINT #2** for dogtooth border, outer border, and flower center appliqués
12 x 14-inch piece	**GOLD PRINT** for pumpkin appliqué
8 x 24-inch piece	**ORANGE PUMPKIN PRINT** for flower petal appliqués
8 x 24-inch piece	**RED PRINT** for flower petal appliqués
8 x 15-inch piece	*each* of **2 GREEN PRINTS** for leaf appliqués
1/2 yard	**GREEN FLORAL** for binding

3-1/4 yards for backing

quilt batting, at least 58-inches square

template material

paper-backed fusible web for appliqué

pearl cotton or machine embroidery thread for decorative stitches: black, gold

tear-away fabric stabilizer (optional)

NOTE: read **Getting Started**, *page 123, before beginning this project.*

Quilt Center

Cutting

From **BEIGE FLORAL:**
- Cut 1, 20-1/2 x 42-inch strip. From the strip cut:
  1, 20-1/2-inch appliqué foundation square
  4, 2-1/2 x 8-1/2-inch rectangles
  8, 2-1/2 x 6-1/2-inch rectangles

From **MEDIUM GREEN PRINT:**
- Cut 5, 2-1/2 x 42-inch strips.
  From 2 of the strips cut:
  28, 2-1/2-inch squares
  The remaining strips will be used
  for the inner border.
  Diagonally piece the strips as needed referring to
  Diagonal Piecing on page 128.

Piecing

Step 1 Position 2-1/2-inch **MEDIUM GREEN** squares on both corners of a 2-1/2 x 8-1/2-inch **BEIGE FLORAL** rectangle. Draw diagonal lines on the squares and stitch on the lines. Trim the seam allowances to 1/4-inch; press.

Make 4

Step 2 Position 2-1/2-inch **MEDIUM GREEN** squares on both corners of a 2-1/2 x 6-1/2-inch **BEIGE FLORAL** rectangle. Draw diagonal lines on the squares; stitch, trim, and press.

Make 8

Step 3 Sew together 1 of the Step 1 units and 2 of the Step 2 units; press. Make 4 pieced border strips. Sew 2 of the pieced border strips to the top/bottom edges of the 20-1/2-inch **BEIGE FLORAL** appliqué foundation square; press. Sew 2-1/2-inch **MEDIUM GREEN** squares to both ends of the remaining pieced border strips; press. Sew the strips to the side edges of the appliqué foundation square; press.

Step 4 Attach the 2-1/2-inch wide **MEDIUM GREEN** inner border strips.

Appliqué Placement Diagram

Fusible Web Appliqué

Step 1 Make templates of the appliqué shapes on pages 69–73. Trace the shapes on the paper side of the fusible web, leaving a small margin between each shape. Cut the shapes apart.

Note: *When you are fusing a large shape, like the pumpkin, fuse just the outer edges of the shape so that it will not look stiff when finished. To do this, draw a line about 3/8-inch inside the pumpkin, and cut away the fusible web on this line.*

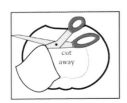
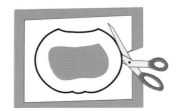

Step 2 Following the manufacturer's instructions, fuse the shapes to the wrong side of the fabrics chosen for the appliqués. Let the fabric cool and cut along the traced line. Peel away the paper backing from the fusible web.

Step 3 Referring to the appliqué placement diagram, position the appliqué shapes on the quilt center, layering them as needed, and fuse in place. We suggest pinning a rectangle of tear-away stabilizer to the backside of the fabric to be appliquéd on so that it will lay flat when the appliqué is complete. We use the extra-lightweight Easy Tear™ sheets as a stabilizer. When the appliqué is complete, tear away the stabilizer.

Step 4 Machine appliqué was used to appliqué the shapes in place. We machine blanket stitched around the shapes using machine embroidery thread for the top thread and regular sewing thread in the bobbin. If you like, you could hand-blanket stitch around the shapes with pearl cotton.

Blanket Stitch

Note: *To prevent the hand blanket stitches from "rolling off" the edges of the appliqué shapes, take an extra backstitch in the same place as you made the blanket stitch, going around outer curves, corners, and points. For straight edges, taking a backstitch every inch is enough.*

Borders

Note: *The yardage given allows for the border strips to be cut on the crosswise grain. Diagonally piece the strips as needed, referring to **Diagonal Piecing** instructions on page 128. Read through **Border** instructions on pages 127–128 for general instructions on adding borders.*

Cutting

From **BLACK PRINT #1:**
• Cut 4, 2-1/2 x 42-inch middle border strips

From **ORANGE FLORAL:**
• Cut 4, 2-1/2 x 42-inch middle border strips

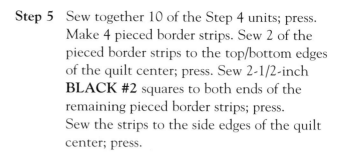

From **MEDIUM GREEN PRINT:**
- Cut 4, 2-1/2 x 42-inch middle border strips
- Cut 5 more 2-1/2 x 42-inch strips
  From the strips cut: 80, 2-1/2-inch squares

From **BLACK PRINT #2:**
- Cut 6, 4-1/2 x 42-inch outer border strips
- Cut 5, 2-1/2 x 42-inch strips
  From the strips cut:
  40, 2-1/2 x 4-1/2-inch rectangles
  4, 2-1/2-inch squares

Attaching the Borders

Step 1 Attach the 2-1/2-inch wide **BLACK #1** middle border strips.

Step 2 Attach the 2-1/2-inch wide **ORANGE FLORAL** middle border strips.

Step 3 Attach the 2-1/2-inch wide **MEDIUM GREEN** middle border strips.

Step 4 Position a 2-1/2-inch **MEDIUM GREEN** square on the corner of a 2-1/2 x 4-1/2-inch **BLACK #2** rectangle. Draw a diagonal line on the square; stitch, trim, and press. Repeat this process at the opposite corner of the rectangle.

Make 40

Step 5 Sew together 10 of the Step 4 units; press. Make 4 pieced border strips. Sew 2 of the pieced border strips to the top/bottom edges of the quilt center; press. Sew 2-1/2-inch **BLACK #2** squares to both ends of the remaining pieced border strips; press. Sew the strips to the side edges of the quilt center; press.

Step 6 Attach the 4-1/2-inch wide **BLACK #2** outer border strips.

Putting It All Together

Cut the 3-1/4 yard length of backing fabric in half crosswise to make 2, 1-5/8 yard lengths. Refer to **Finishing the Quilt** on page 128 for complete instructions.

Binding

Cutting

From **GREEN FLORAL:**
- Cut 6, 2-3/4 x 42-inch strips

Sew the binding to the quilt using a 3/8-inch seam allowance. This measurement will produce a 1/2-inch wide finished double binding. Refer to **Binding** and **Diagonal Piecing** on page 128 for complete instructions.

Small Leaf

Trace 2 onto fusible web

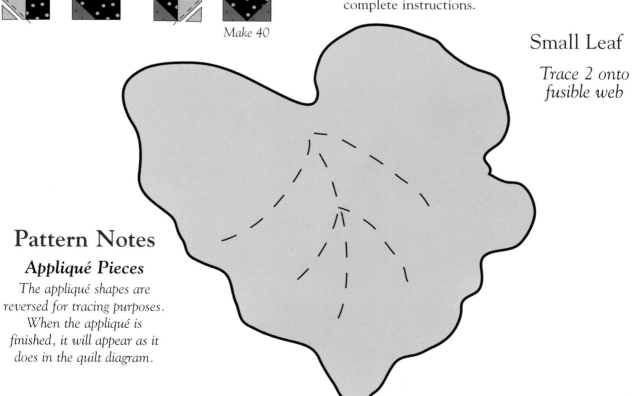

Pattern Notes

Appliqué Pieces

The appliqué shapes are reversed for tracing purposes. When the appliqué is finished, it will appear as it does in the quilt diagram.

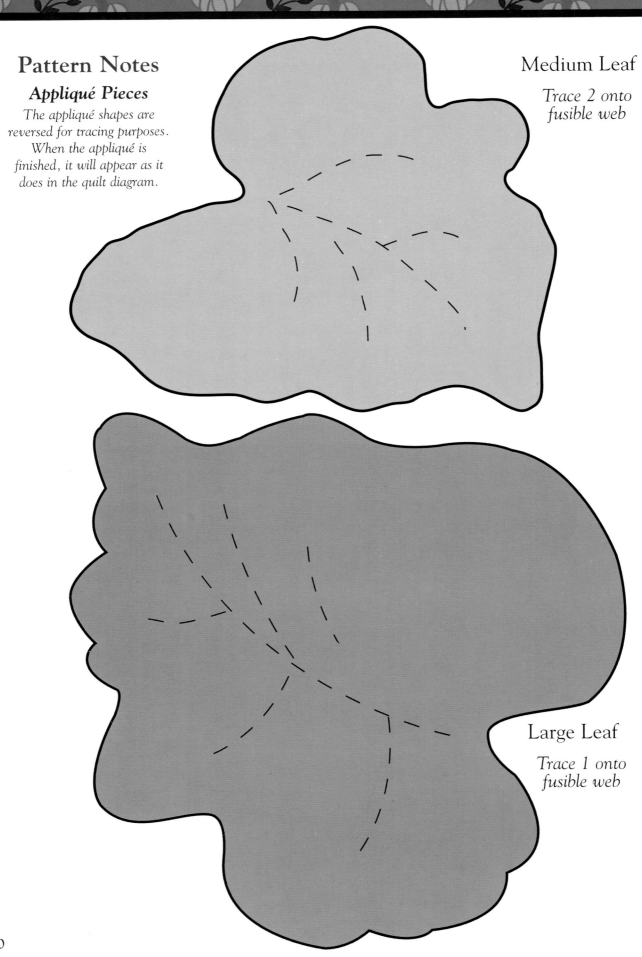

Pattern Notes

Appliqué Pieces

The appliqué shapes are reversed for tracing purposes. When the appliqué is finished, it will appear as it does in the quilt diagram.

Medium Leaf

Trace 2 onto fusible web

Large Leaf

Trace 1 onto fusible web

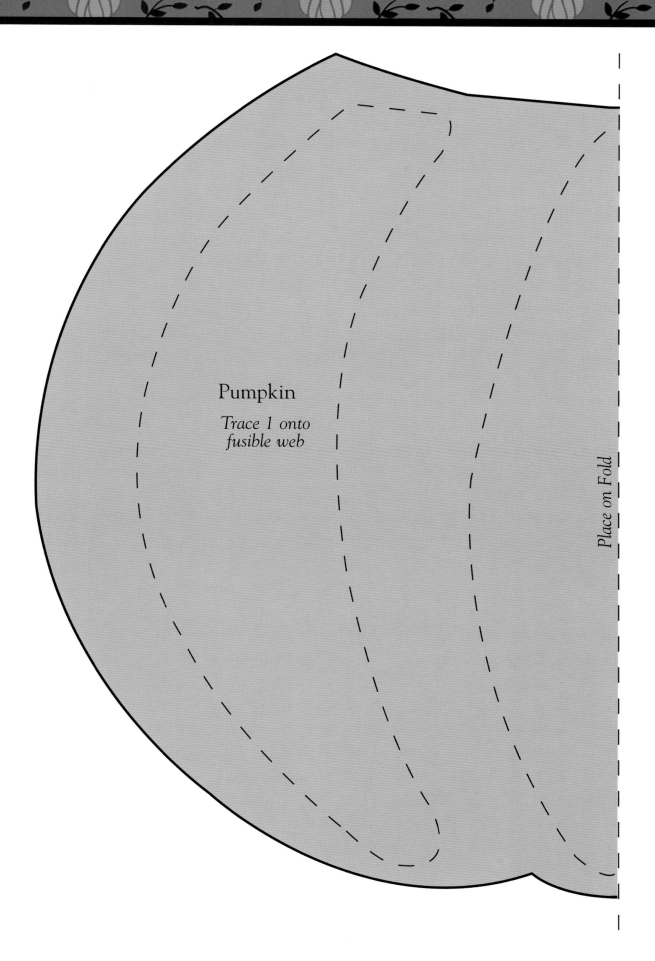

Pumpkin

Trace 1 onto fusible web

Place on Fold

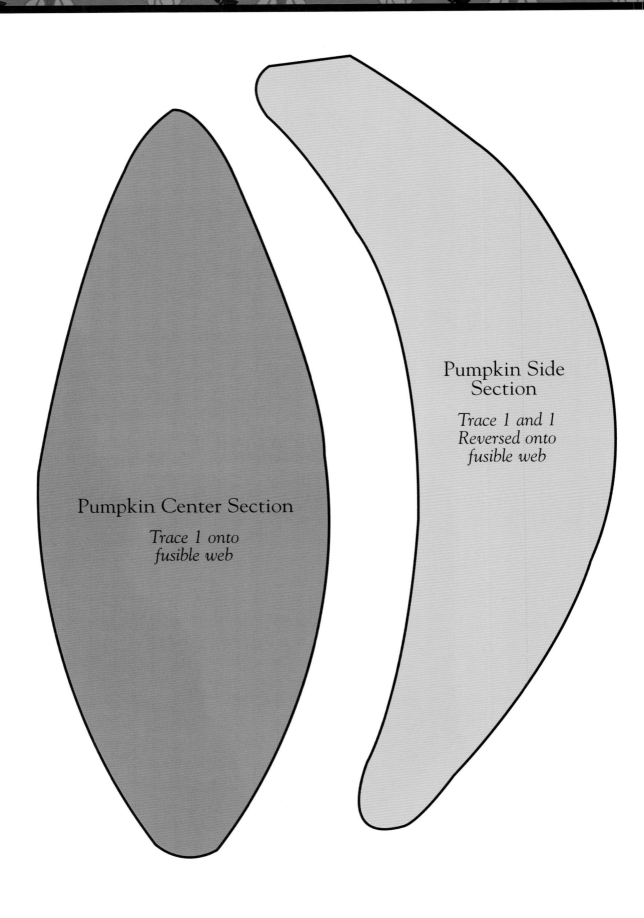

Pumpkin Side
Section

Trace 1 and 1
Reversed onto
fusible web

Pumpkin Center Section

Trace 1 onto
fusible web

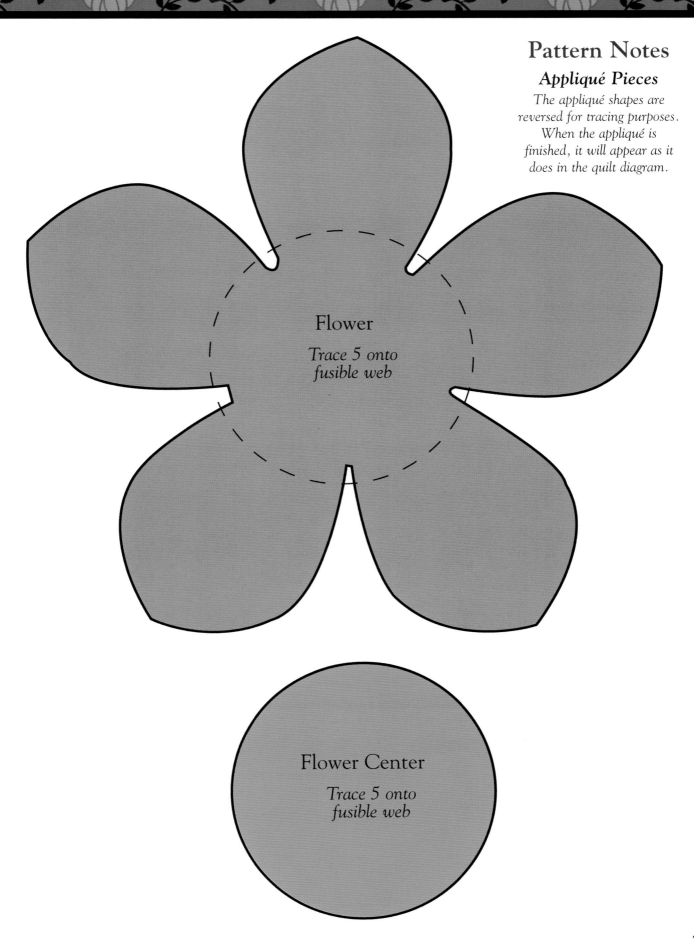

Pattern Notes

Appliqué Pieces

The appliqué shapes are reversed for tracing purposes. When the appliqué is finished, it will appear as it does in the quilt diagram.

Flower

Trace 5 onto fusible web

Flower Center

Trace 5 onto fusible web

Pumpkin Blossom Wall Quilt
52-inches square

A wire plant rack with pots filled to overflowing with mums, fall foliage and a trio of pumpkins is an impressive tribute to autumn.

Pumpkin Patch

Stars take center stage on the cream-and-black-themed wall quilt and harvest display.

 Wall Quilt

32 x 46-inches

Fabrics & Supplies

1/8 yard	**ORANGE PRINT #1** for pumpkin block (outer sections)
1/8 yard	**RED FLORAL** for pumpkin block (middle sections)
6 x 14-inch piece	**ORANGE PRINT #2** for pumpkin block (center section)
1/3 yard	**GREEN PRINT** for stem and inner border
1/2 yard	**BEIGE PRINT** for background
1/4 yard	**BLACK PRINT** for star points and middle border
1/8 yard	**LIGHT GOLD PRINT** for star points
6-inch square	**DARK GOLD PRINT** for star center
7/8 yard	**CHESTNUT FLORAL** for outer border
1/3 yard	**BLACK PRINT** for binding

1-3/8 yards for backing

quilt batting, at least 38 x 52-inches

NOTE: read **Getting Started**, page 123, before beginning this project.

Pumpkin Block

Makes 1 block
Cutting
From **ORANGE PRINT #1** (outer sections):
- Cut 1, 2-1/2 x 42-inch strip. From the strip cut:
  2, 2-1/2 x 12-1/2-inch rectangles
  4, 2-1/2-inch squares

From **RED FLORAL** (middle sections):
- Cut 1, 2-1/2 x 42-inch strip. From the strip cut:
  2, 2-1/2 x 12-1/2-inch rectangles
  4, 2-1/2-inch squares

From **ORANGE PRINT #2** (center section):
- Cut 1, 4-1/2 x 12-1/2-inch rectangle

From **BEIGE PRINT:**
- Cut 1, 4-1/2 x 42-inch strip. From the strip cut:
  1, 4-1/2 x 6-1/2-inch rectangle
  1, 4-1/2 x 5-1/2-inch rectangle
  4, 2-1/2-inch squares
  1, 1-1/2-inch square

From **GREEN PRINT:**
- Cut 1, 2-1/2-inch square
- Cut 1, 1-1/2 x 4-1/2-inch rectangle

Piecing

Step 1 With right sides together, position 2-1/2-inch **BEIGE** squares on both corners of a 2-1/2 x 12-1/2-inch **ORANGE #1** rectangle. Draw diagonal lines on the squares and stitch on the lines. Trim the seam allowances to 1/4-inch; press.

Make 2

Step 2 Position 2-1/2-inch **ORANGE #1** squares on both corners of a 2-1/2 x 12-1/2-inch **RED FLORAL** rectangle. Draw diagonal lines on the squares; stitch, trim, and press.

Make 2

Step 3 Position 2-1/2-inch **RED FLORAL** squares on 2 opposite corners of the 4-1/2 x 12-1/2-inch **ORANGE #2** rectangle. Draw diagonal lines on the squares; stitch, trim, and press. Repeat this process for the remaining corners of the rectangle.

Make 1

Step 4 Referring to the pumpkin block diagram, sew the Step 1, 2, and 3 units together; press to make the pumpkin unit.

Step 5 Position the 2-1/2-inch **GREEN** square on the corner of the 4-1/2 x 6-1/2-inch **BEIGE** rectangle. Draw a diagonal line on the square; stitch, trim, and press.

Make 1

Step 6 Position the 1-1/2-inch **BEIGE** square on the corner of the 1-1/2 x 4-1/2-inch **GREEN** rectangle. Draw a diagonal line on the square; stitch, trim, and press.

Make 1

Step 7 Referring to the pumpkin block diagram, sew the Step 5 and 6 units together. Sew the 4-1/2 x 5-1/2-inch **BEIGE** rectangle to the right edge of this unit; press to make a stem unit. Sew the stem unit to the top edge of the pumpkin unit; press. <u>At this point the pumpkin block should measure 12-1/2 x 16-1/2-inches.</u>

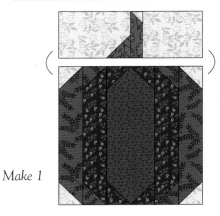

Make 1

Star Block

Makes 1 block
Cutting

From **BLACK PRINT:**
- Cut 1, 2-1/2 x 42-inch strip. From the strip cut:
  4, 2-1/2 x 4-1/2-inch rectangles
  8, 2-1/2-inch squares

From **LIGHT GOLD PRINT:**
- Cut 1, 2-1/2 x 42-inch strip. From the strip cut:
  8, 2-1/2-inch squares

From **DARK GOLD PRINT:**
- Cut 1, 4-1/2-inch square

From **BEIGE PRINT:**
- Cut 1, 4-1/2 x 42-inch strip. From the strip cut:
  4, 4-1/2-inch squares
  4, 2-1/2 x 4-1/2-inch rectangles

Piecing

Step 1 With right sides together, position a 2-1/2-inch **BLACK** square on the corner of a 2-1/2 x 4-1/2-inch **BEIGE** rectangle. Draw a diagonal line on the square; stitch, trim, and press. Repeat this process at the opposite corner of the rectangle.

Make 4

Step 2 Position a 2-1/2-inch **LIGHT GOLD** square on the corner of a 2-1/2 x 4-1/2-inch **BLACK** rectangle. Draw a diagonal line on the square; stitch, trim, and press. Repeat this process at the opposite corner of the rectangle. Sew the unit to the bottom edge of the Step 1 unit; press. <u>At this point each unit should measure 4-1/2-inches square.</u>

Make 4   *Make 4*

Step 3 Sew Step 2 units to both side edges of the 4-1/2-inch **DARK GOLD** square; press. <u>At this point the unit should measure 4-1/2 x 12-1/2-inches.</u>

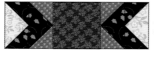

Make 1

Step 4 Sew 4-1/2-inch **BEIGE** squares to both side edges of the remaining Step 2 units; press. <u>At this point each unit should measure 4-1/2 x 12-1/2-inches.</u>

Make 2

Step 5 Sew the Step 4 units to the top/bottom edges of the Step 3 unit; press. <u>At this point the star block should measure 12-1/2-inches square.</u>

Make 1

Quilt Center

Cutting

From **BEIGE PRINT:**
- Cut 2 to 3, 2-1/2 x 42-inch strips.
  From the strips cut:
  2, 2-1/2 x 30-1/2-inch strips
  1, 2-1/2 x 12-1/2-inch strip

Quilt Center Assembly

Step 1 Sew the pumpkin block to the bottom edge of the star block; press. <u>At this point the quilt center should measure 12-1/2 x 28-1/2-inches.</u>

Step 2 Sew the 2-1/2 x 12-1/2-inch **BEIGE** strip to the top edge of the quilt center; press. Sew the 2-1/2 x 30-1/2-inch **BEIGE** strips to the side edges of the quilt center; press.

Borders

Note: *The yardage given allows for the border strips to be cut on the crosswise grain. Diagonally piece the strips as needed, referring to* **Diagonal Piecing** *on page 128 for complete instructions. Read through* **Border** *instructions on pages 127–128 for general instructions on adding borders.*

Cutting

From **GREEN PRINT:**
- Cut 3, 2-1/2 x 42-inch inner border strips

From **BLACK PRINT:**
- Cut 3, 1-1/2 x 42-inch middle border strips

From **CHESTNUT FLORAL:**
- Cut 5, 5-1/2 x 42-inch outer border strips

Attaching the Borders

Step 1 Attach the 2-1/2-inch wide **GREEN** inner border strips.

Step 2 Attach the 1-1/2-inch wide **BLACK** middle border strips.

Step 3 Attach the 5-1/2-inch wide **CHESTNUT FLORAL** outer border strips.

Putting It All Together

Trim the backing and batting so they are 6-inches larger than the quilt top. Refer to **Finishing the Quilt** on page 128 for complete instructions.

Binding

Cutting

From **BLACK PRINT:**
• Cut 4, 2-3/4 x 42-inch strips

Sew the binding to the quilt using a 3/8-inch seam allowance. This measurement will produce a 1/2-inch wide finished double binding. Refer to **Binding** and **Diagonal Piecing** on page 00 for complete instructions.

Pumpkin Patch Wall Quilt
32 x 46-inches

Topping off an unlidded black cookie jar with a Jack Frost
pumpkin casts an eerie shadow of candlelight against the wall.

Pumpkin Patch

Quick treats are no trick at all when you combine them all into a tasteful celebration of Halloween.

Table Runner

20 x 52-inches

Fabrics & Supplies

1/4 yard	**ORANGE PRINT #1** for pumpkin blocks (outer sections)
1/4 yard	**ORANGE PRINT #2** for pumpkin blocks (middle sections)
1/4 yard	**ORANGE PRINT #3** for pumpkin blocks (center section)
1/3 yard	**GREEN PRINT** for stems and inner border
3/8 yard	**BEIGE PRINT** for background
1/8 yard	**BLACK PRINT** for star points
1/8 yard	**DARK GOLD PRINT** for star points
6-inch square	**MEDIUM GOLD PRINT** for star center
1/2 yard	**RUST W/ GOLD FLORAL** for outer border
3/8 yard	**BLACK PRINT** for binding

1-5/8 yards for backing

quilt batting, at least 26 x 58-inches

NOTE: read **Getting Started**, page 123, before beginning this project.

Pumpkin Block

Makes 2 blocks

Cutting

From **ORANGE PRINT #1** (outer sections):
- Cut 2, 2-1/2 x 42-inch strips.
  From the strips cut:
  4, 2-1/2 x 12-1/2-inch rectangles
  8, 2-1/2-inch squares

From **ORANGE PRINT #2** (middle sections):
- Cut 2, 2-1/2 x 42-inch strips.
  From the strips cut:
  4, 2-1/2 x 12-1/2-inch rectangles
  8, 2-1/2-inch squares

From **ORANGE PRINT #3** (center section):
- Cut 1, 4-1/2 x 42-inch strip.
  From the strip cut:
  2, 4-1/2 x 12-1/2-inch rectangles

From **BEIGE PRINT:**
- Cut 1, 4-1/2 x 42-inch strip.
  From the strip cut:
  2, 4-1/2 x 6-1/2-inch rectangles
  2, 4-1/2 x 5-1/2-inch rectangles
- Cut 1, 2-1/2 x 42-inch strip.
  From the strip cut:
  8, 2-1/2-inch squares
  2, 1-1/2-inch squares

From **GREEN PRINT:**
- Cut 2, 2-1/2-inch squares
- Cut 2, 1-1/2 x 4-1/2-inch rectangles

Piecing

Step 1 With right sides together, position 2-1/2-inch **BEIGE** squares on both corners of a 2-1/2 x 12-1/2-inch **ORANGE #1** rectangle. Draw diagonal lines on the squares and stitch on the lines. Trim the seam allowances to 1/4-inch; press.

Make 4

Step 2 Position 2-1/2-inch **ORANGE #1** squares on both corners of a 2-1/2 x 12-1/2-inch **ORANGE #2** rectangle. Draw diagonal lines on the squares; stitch, trim, and press.

Make 4

Step 3 Position 2-1/2-inch **ORANGE #2** squares on 2 opposite corners of a 4-1/2 x 12-1/2-inch **ORANGE #3** rectangle. Draw diagonal lines on the squares; stitch, trim, and press. Repeat this process for the remaining corners of the rectangle.

Make 2

Step 4 Referring to the pumpkin block diagram for placement, sew the Step 1, 2, and 3 units together; press to make the pumpkin unit. Make 2 units.

Step 5 Position a 2-1/2-inch **GREEN** square on the corner of a 4-1/2 x 6-1/2-inch **BEIGE** rectangle. Draw a diagonal line on the square; stitch, trim, and press.

Make 2

Step 6 Position a 1-1/2-inch **BEIGE** square on the corner of a 1-1/2 x 4-1/2-inch **GREEN** rectangle. Draw a diagonal line on the square; stitch, trim, and press.

Make 2

Step 7 Referring to the pumpkin block diagram, sew the Step 5 and 6 units together. Sew a 4-1/2 x 5-1/2-inch **BEIGE** rectangle to the right edge of this unit; press to make a stem unit. Sew the stem unit to the top edge of the Step 4 pumpkin unit; press. <u>At this point each pumpkin block should measure 12-1/2 x 16-1/2-inches.</u>

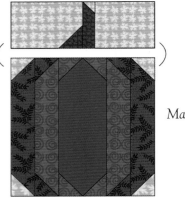

Make 2

Star Block

Makes 1 block

Cutting

From **BLACK PRINT**:
- Cut 1, 2-1/2 x 42-inch strip. From the strip cut:
  4, 2-1/2 x 4-1/2-inch rectangles
  8, 2-1/2-inch squares

From **DARK GOLD PRINT**:
- Cut 1, 2-1/2 x 42-inch strip. From the strip cut:
  8, 2-1/2-inch squares

From **MEDIUM GOLD PRINT**:
- Cut 1, 4-1/2-inch square

From **BEIGE PRINT**:
- Cut 1, 4-1/2 x 42-inch strip. From the strip cut:
  4, 4-1/2-inch squares
  4, 2-1/2 x 4-1/2-inch rectangles

Piecing

Step 1 With right sides together, position a 2-1/2-inch **BLACK** square on the corner of a 2-1/2 x 4-1/2-inch **BEIGE** rectangle. Draw a diagonal line on the square; stitch, trim, and press. Repeat this process at the opposite corner of the rectangle.

Make 4

Step 2 Position a 2-1/2-inch **DARK GOLD** square on the corner of a 2-1/2 x 4-1/2-inch **BLACK** rectangle. Draw a diagonal line on the square; stitch, trim, and press. Repeat this process at the opposite corner of the rectangle. Sew the unit to the bottom edge of a Step 1 unit; press. At this point each unit should measure 4-1/2-inches square.

Make 4   *Make 4*

Step 3 Sew Step 2 units to both side edges of the 4-1/2-inch **MEDIUM GOLD** square; press. At this point the unit should measure 4-1/2 x 12-1/2-inches.

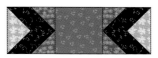

Make 1

Step 4 Sew 4-1/2-inch **BEIGE** squares to both side edges of the remaining Step 2 units; press. At this point each unit should measure 4-1/2 x 12-1/2-inches.

Make 2

Step 5 Sew the Step 4 units to the top/bottom edges of the Step 3 unit; press. At this point the star block should measure 12-1/2-inches square.

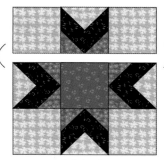

Make 1

Step 6 Sew the pumpkin blocks to both side edges of the star block; press.

Borders

Note: *The yardage given allows for the border strips to be cut on the crosswise grain. Diagonally piece the strips as needed, referring to* **Diagonal Piecing** *on page 128 for complete instructions. Read through* **Border** *instructions on pages 127–128 for general instructions on adding borders.*

Cutting

From **GREEN PRINT:**
• Cut 4, 1-1/2 x 42-inch inner border strips

From **RUST w/ GOLD FLORAL:**
• Cut 4, 3-1/2 x 42-inch outer border strips

Attaching the Borders

Step 1 Attach the 1-1/2-inch wide **GREEN** inner border strips.

Step 2 Attach the 3-1/2-inch wide **RUST w/GOLD FLORAL** outer border strips.

Putting It All Together

Trim the backing and batting so they are 6-inches larger than the runner top. Refer to **Finishing the Quilt** on page 128 for complete instructions.

Binding

Cutting

From **BLACK PRINT:**
• Cut 4, 2-3/4 x 42-inch strips

Sew the binding to the quilt using a 3/8-inch seam allowance. This measurement will produce a 1/2-inch wide finished double binding. Refer to **Binding** and **Diagonal Piecing** on page 128 for complete instructions.

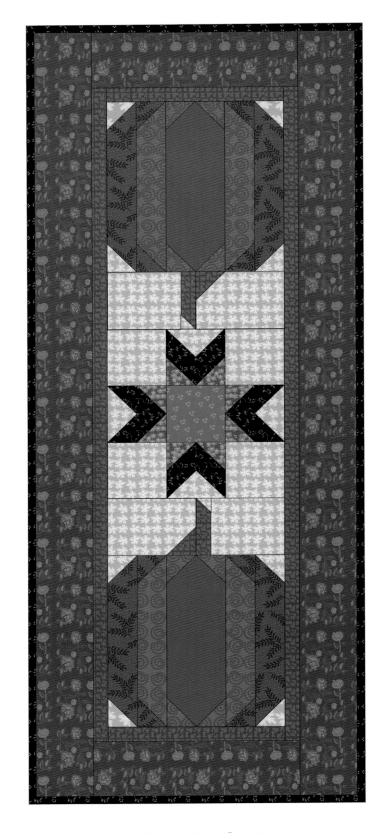

Pumpkin Patch Table Runner

20 x 52-inches

Antique and reproduction memorabilia provide more than grins
for serious collectors—Halloween history has lasting value!

Sugarhouse Pumpkin

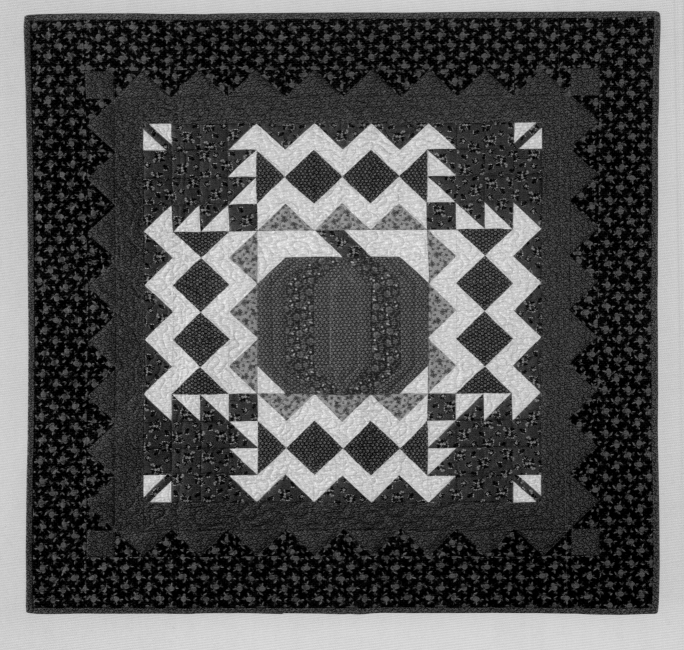

A Sugarhouse pumpkin goes solo in a glowing tribute to the splendor of the season.

Wall Quilt

44-inches square

Fabrics & Supplies

1/4 yard	**RUST PRINT** for pumpkin block
1/8 yard	**RED FLORAL** for pumpkin block
5/8 yard	**GREEN PRINT** for pumpkin stem, leaf blocks, and middle dogtooth sections
7/8 yard	**BEIGE PRINT** for background
1/4 yard	**GOLD PRINT** for inner dogtooth sections
1/3 yard	**PURPLE/GREEN PRINT** for diamond sections
2/3 yard	**BROWN PRINT** for inner border, outer dogtooth border, and corner squares
1-1/8 yards	**PURPLE/GOLD FLORAL** for outer dogtooth and outer borders
1/2 yard	**BROWN PRINT** for binding

2-3/4 yards for backing

quilt batting, at least 50-inches square

NOTE: read **Getting Started**, page 123, before beginning this project.

Pumpkin Block

Makes 1 block
Cutting

From **RUST PRINT**:
• Cut 1, 4-1/2 x 42-inch strip. From the strip cut:
  1, 4-1/2 x 10-1/2-inch rectangle
  2, 2-1/2 x 10-1/2-inch rectangles
  4, 2-1/2-inch squares

From **RED FLORAL**:
• Cut 1, 2-1/2 x 42-inch strip. From the strip cut:
  2, 2-1/2 x 10-1/2-inch rectangles
  4, 2-1/2-inch squares

From **GREEN PRINT**:
• Cut 2, 2-1/2-inch squares

From **BEIGE PRINT**:
• Cut 1, 2-1/2 x 42-inch strip. From the strip cut:
  2, 2-1/2 x 6-1/2-inch rectangles
  4, 2-1/2-inch squares

Piecing

Step 1 With right sides together, position 2-1/2-inch **BEIGE** squares on the corners of a 2-1/2 x 10-1/2-inch **RUST** rectangle. Draw a diagonal line on the squares and stitch on the lines. Trim the seam allowances to 1/4-inch; press.

Make 2

Step 2 Position 2-1/2-inch **RUST** squares on the corners of a 2-1/2 x 10-1/2-inch **RED FLORAL** rectangle. Draw a diagonal line on the squares; stitch, trim, and press.

Make 2

Step 3 Position 2-1/2-inch **RED FLORAL** squares on 2 opposite corners of a 4-1/2 x 10-1/2-inch **RUST** rectangle. Draw a diagonal line on the squares; stitch, trim, and press. Repeat this process for the remaining corners of the rectangle.

 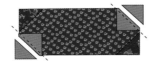

Make 1

Step 4 Referring to the Step 6 block diagram, sew the Step 1, 2, and 3 units together; press. <u>At this point the pumpkin section should measure 10-1/2 x 12-1/2-inches.</u>

Step 5 Position a 2-1/2-inch **GREEN** square on the right corner of a 2-1/2 x 6-1/2-inch **BEIGE** rectangle. Draw a diagonal line on the square; stitch, trim, and press. Make 2 units. Sew the units together; press. <u>At this point the stem section should measure 2-1/2 x 12-1/2-inches.</u>

Make 2   *Make 1*

Step 6 Sew the Step 5 stem section to the top edge of the Step 4 pumpkin section to complete the pumpkin block. <u>At this point the pumpkin block should measure 12-1/2-inches square.</u>

Make 1

Leaf Blocks

Makes 4 blocks

Cutting

From **GREEN PRINT:**
- Cut 1, 2-7/8 x 20-inch strip
- Cut 3, 2-1/2 x 42-inch strips. From the strips cut:
  8, 2-1/2 x 8-1/2-inch rectangles
  4, 2-1/2 x 6-1/2-inch rectangles
  4, 2-1/2-inch squares
  4, 1 x 4-1/2-inch stem strips

From **BEIGE PRINT:**
- Cut 1, 2-7/8 x 20-inch strip
- Cut 4, 2-5/8-inch squares. Cut each square in half diagonally to make 8 triangles.
- Cut 1, 2-1/2 x 42-inch strip. From the strip cut:
  12, 2-1/2-inch squares

Piecing

Step 1 With right sides together, layer the 2-7/8 x 20-inch **GREEN** and **BEIGE** strips together in pairs. Press together, but do not sew. Cut the layered strips into squares. Cut the layered squares in half diagonally to make 12 sets of triangles. Stitch 1/4-inch from the diagonal edge of each pair of triangles; press.

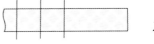

Crosscut 6, 2-7/8-inch squares

Make 12, 2-1/2-inch triangle-pieced squares

Step 2 Sew 3 of the triangle-pieced squares together; press. Sew a 2-1/2-inch **GREEN** square to the left edge of the unit; press. <u>At this point each unit should measure 2-1/2 x 8-1/2-inches.</u>

Make 4

Step 3 Position a 2-1/2-inch **BEIGE** square on the left corner of a 2-1/2 x 8-1/2-inch **GREEN** rectangle. Draw a diagonal line on the square; stitch, trim, and press. Make 8

units. Sew the units together in pairs; press. <u>At this point each unit should measure 4-1/2 x 8-1/2-inches.</u>

Make 8

Make 4

Step 4 Position a 2-1/2-inch **BEIGE** square on the left corner of a 2-1/2 x 6-1/2-inch **GREEN** rectangle. Draw a diagonal line on the square; stitch, trim, and press.

 Make 4

Step 5 To make the stem unit, center a **BEIGE** triangle on a 1 x 4-1/2-inch **GREEN** strip; stitch a 1/4-inch seam. Center another **BEIGE** triangle on the opposite edge of the strip; stitch and press. <u>Trim the stem unit so it measures 2-1/2-inches square.</u> Make 4 stem units. Sew the stem units to the right edge of the Step 4 units; press. <u>At this point each unit should measure 2-1/2 x 8-1/2-inches.</u>

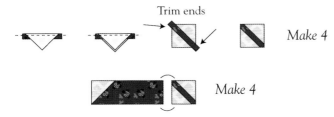

Trim ends

Make 4

Make 4

Step 6 Sew the Step 2, 3, and 5 units together; press to make the leaf blocks. <u>At this point each leaf block should measure 8-1/2-inches square.</u>

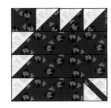

Make 4

Quilt Center

Cutting

From BEIGE PRINT:
- Cut 6, 2-1/2 x 42-inch strips. From the strips cut: 96, 2-1/2-inch squares

From GOLD PRINT:
- Cut 2, 2-1/2 x 42-inch strips. From the strips cut: 12, 2-1/2 x 4-1/2-inch rectangles

From PURPLE/GREEN PRINT:
- Cut 3, 2-1/2 x 42-inch strips. From the strips cut: 24, 2-1/2 x 4-1/2-inch rectangles

From GREEN PRINT:
- Cut 2, 2-1/2 x 42-inch strips. From the strips cut: 12, 2-1/2 x 4-1/2-inch rectangles

Piecing

Step 1 With right sides together, position a 2-1/2-inch **BEIGE** square on the corner of a 2-1/2 x 4-1/2-inch **GOLD** rectangle. Draw a diagonal line on the square; stitch, trim, and press. Repeat this process at the opposite corner of the rectangle. Sew the units together in 4 sections of 3 each; press. <u>At this point each inner dogtooth section should measure 2-1/2 x 12-1/2-inches.</u>

  Make 12

Make 4

Step 2 Repeat Step 1 using the 2-1/2-inch **BEIGE** squares and the 2-1/2 x 4-1/2-inch **GREEN** rectangles. Sew the units together in 4 sections of 3 each; press. <u>At this point each middle dogtooth section should measure 2-1/2 x 12-1/2-inches.</u>

Make 4   *Make 4*

Step 3 Repeat Step 1 using the 2-1/2-inch **BEIGE** squares and the 2-1/2 x 4-1/2-inch **PURPLE/GREEN** rectangles. Referring to the diagram, sew the units together in 4 sections of 6 each; press. <u>At this point each diamond section should measure 4-1/2 x 12-1/2-inches.</u>

Make 24   *Make 4*

Step 4 Referring to the diagram for placement, sew together the Step 1, 2, and 3 dogtooth/diamond sections; press. At this point each section should measure 8-1/2 x 12-1/2-inches.

Make 4

Step 5 Referring to the quilt diagram for block placement, sew Step 4 sections to the top/bottom edges of the pumpkin block; press. At this point the section should measure 12-1/2 x 28-1/2-inches.

Step 6 Referring to the quilt diagram for block placement, sew leaf blocks to the side edges of the remaining Step 4 dogtooth/diamond sections; press. Make 2 sections. At this point each section should measure 8-1/2 x 28-1/2-inches.

Step 7 Sew the Step 6 sections to the side edges of the quilt center; press. At this point the quilt center should measure 28-1/2-inches square.

Borders

*Note: The yardage given allows for the border strips to be cut on the crosswise grain. Diagonally piece the strips as needed, referring to **Diagonal Piecing** instructions on page 128. Read through **Border** instructions on pages 127–128 for general instructions on adding borders.*

Cutting

From BROWN PRINT:
- Cut 4, 2-1/2 x 42-inch inner border strips
- Cut 4 more 2-1/2 x 42-inch strips.
  From the strips cut:
  32, 2-1/2 x 4-1/2-inch rectangles
  4, 2-1/2-inch corner squares

From PURPLE/GOLD FLORAL:
- Cut 5, 4-1/2 x 42-inch outer border strips
- Cut 4, 2-1/2 x 42-inch strips. From the strips cut:
  64, 2-1/2-inch squares

Assembling and Attaching the Borders

Step 1 Attach the 2-1/2-inch wide **BROWN** inner border strips.

Step 2 Position a 2-1/2-inch **PURPLE/GREEN FLORAL** square on the corner of a 2-1/2 x 4-1/2-inch **BROWN** rectangle. Draw a diagonal line on the square; stitch, trim, and press. Repeat this process at the opposite corner of the rectangle.

Make 32

Step 3 For the top/bottom dogtooth borders, sew together 8 of the Step 2 units; press. Make 2 border strips. At this point each dogtooth border strip should measure 2-1/2 x 32-1/2-inches. Sew the border strips to the quilt center; press.

Step 4 Repeat Step 3 for the side dogtooth borders, adding 2-1/2-inch **BROWN** corner squares to both ends of the border strips; press. Make 2 border strips. At this point each dogtooth border strip should measure 2-1/2 x 36-1/2-inches. Sew the border strips to the quilt center; press.

Step 5 Attach the 4-1/2-inch wide **PURPLE/GOLD FLORAL** outer border strips.

Putting It All Together

Cut the 2-3/4 yard length of backing fabric in half crosswise to make 2, 1-3/8 yard lengths. Refer to **Finishing the Quilt** on page 128 for complete instructions.

Binding

Cutting

From BROWN PRINT:
- Cut 5, 2-3/4 x 42-inch strips

Sew the binding to the quilt using a 3/8-inch seam allowance. This measurement will produce a 1/2-inch wide finished double binding. Refer to **Binding** and **Diagonal Piecing** on page 128 for complete instructions.

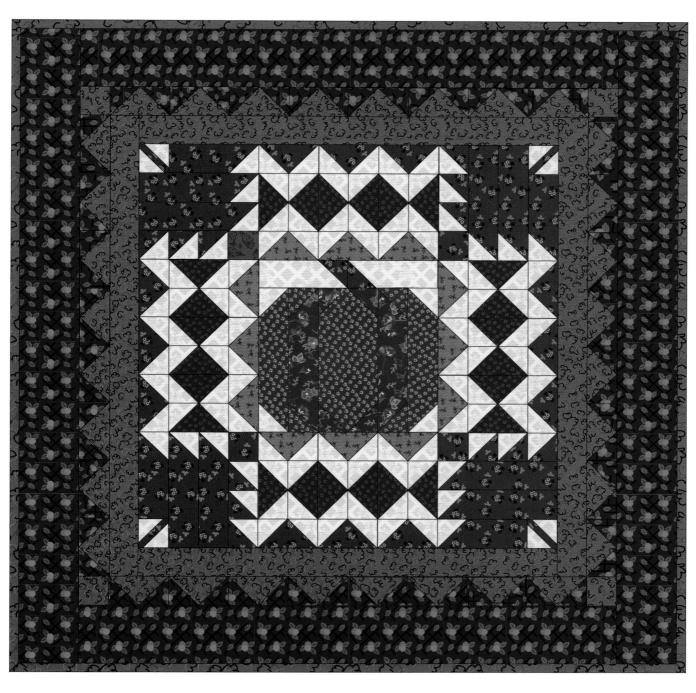

Sugarhouse Pumpkin Wall Quilt
44-inches square

Merry Halloween

For an easy, no-bake treat, fill a plate with peanut butter cookie ghosts dipped in candy coating.

Quilt

52 x 60-inches

Fabrics & Supplies

5/8 yard	**GOLD PRINT** for pieced blocks and dogtooth borders
5/8 yard	**GREEN PRINT** for pieced blocks
1/3 yard	**RED PRINT** for pieced blocks
7/8 yard	**LARGE BLACK FLORAL** for alternate blocks
1-5/8 yards	**RED/GREEN LEAF PRINT** for pieced border and outer border
1/2 yard	**BLACK PRINT** for binding

3-1/4 yards for backing

quilt batting, at least 58 x 66-inches

NOTE: read **Getting Started**,
page 123, before beginning this project.

Pieced Blocks

Makes 13 blocks

Cutting

From **GOLD PRINT:**
* Cut 4, 2-1/2 x 42-inch strips

From **GREEN PRINT:**
* Cut 2, 4-1/2 x 42-inch strips
* Cut 4, 2-1/2 x 42-inch strips

From **RED PRINT:**
* Cut 2, 4-1/2 x 42-inch strips

Piecing

Step 1   Aligning long edges, sew a 2-1/2 x 42-inch **GOLD** strip to both side edges of a 4-1/2 x 42-inch **GREEN** strip. Press the seam allowances toward the **GREEN** strips, referring to **Hints and Helps for Pressing Strip Sets** on page 97. Make 2 strip sets. Cut the strip sets into segments.

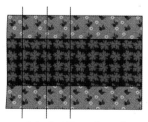

Crosscut 26, 2-1/2-inch wide segments

Step 2 Aligning long edges, sew a 2-1/2 x 42-inch **GREEN** strip to both side edges of a 4-1/2 x 42-inch **RED** strip. Press the seam allowances toward the **GREEN** strips. Make 2 strip sets. Cut the strip sets into segments.

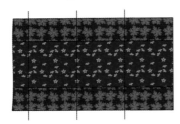

Crosscut 13, 4-1/2-inch wide segments

Step 3 Sew Step 1 units to both side edges of a Step 2 unit; press. <u>At this point each pieced block should measure 8-1/2-inches square.</u>

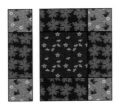

Make 13

Quilt Center

Cutting

From **LARGE BLACK FLORAL:**
- Cut 3, 8-1/2 x 42-inch strips.
  From the strips cut:
  12, 8-1/2-inch alternate block squares

Quilt Center Assembly

Step 1 Referring to the quilt diagram for placement, sew together the pieced blocks and alternate blocks in 5 rows of 5 blocks each. Press the seam allowances toward the alternate blocks.

Step 2 Pin the rows together at the block intersections; sew. Press the seam allowances in one direction. <u>At this point the quilt center should measure 40-1/2-inches square.</u>

Borders

Note: *The yardage given allows for the border strips to be cut on the crosswise grain. Diagonally piece the strips as needed, referring to* **Diagonal Piecing** *on page 128 for*

complete instructions. Read through **Border** instructions on pages 127–128 for general instructions on adding borders.

Cutting

From **RED/GREEN LEAF PRINT:**
- Cut 6, 6-1/2 x 42-inch outer border strips
- Cut 2, 2-1/2 x 42-inch inner border strips
- Cut 3 more 2-1/2 x 42-inch strips.
  From the strips cut:
  40, 2-1/2-inch squares

From **GOLD PRINT:**
- Cut 3, 2-1/2 x 42-inch strips. From the strips cut:
  20, 2-1/2 x 4-1/2-inch rectangles

Assembling and Attaching the Borders

Step 1 Attach the 2-1/2-inch wide **RED/GREEN LEAF PRINT** inner border strips.

Step 2 With right sides together, position a 2-1/2-inch **RED/GREEN LEAF PRINT** square on the corner of a 2-1/2 x 4-1/2-inch **GOLD** rectangle. Draw a diagonal line on the square and stitch on the line. Trim the seam allowance to 1/4-inch; press. Repeat this process at the opposite corner of the rectangle.

Make 20

Step 3 For the top/bottom dogtooth borders, sew together 10 of the Step 2 units; press. Make 2 border strips. Sew the dogtooth borders to the top/bottom edges of the quilt center; press.

Step 4 Attach the 6-1/2-inch wide **RED/GREEN LEAF PRINT** outer border strips.

Putting It All Together

Cut the 3-1/4 yard length of backing fabric in half crosswise to make 2, 1-5/8 yard lengths. Refer to **Finishing the Quilt** on page 128 for complete instructions.

Binding

Cutting

From **BLACK PRINT:**
- Cut 6, 2-3/4 x 42-inch strips

Sew the binding to the quilt using a 3/8-inch seam allowance. This measurement will produce a 1/2-inch wide finished double binding. Refer to **Binding** and **Diagonal Piecing** on page 128 for complete instructions.

Hints and Helps for Pressing Strip Sets

When sewing strips of fabric together for strip sets, it is important to press the seam allowances nice and flat, usually to the dark fabric. Be careful not to stretch as you press, causing a "rainbow effect." This will affect the accuracy and shape of the pieces cut from the strip set. Press on the wrong side first with the strips perpendicular to the ironing board. Flip the piece over and press on the right side to prevent little pleats from forming at the seams. Laying the strip set lengthwise on the ironing board seems to encourage the rainbow effect.

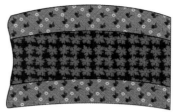

"Avoid this rainbow effect"

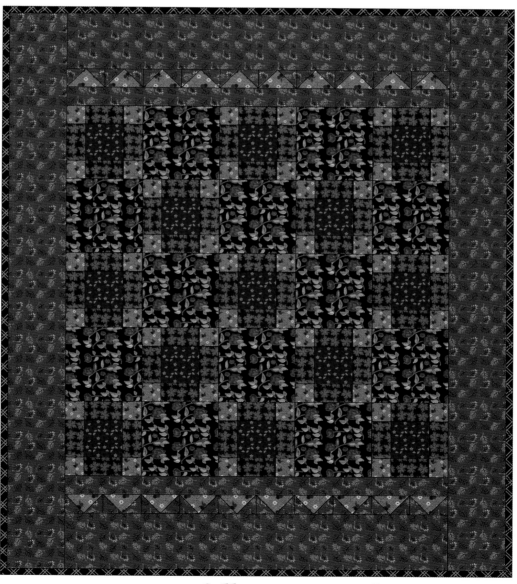

Merry Halloween Quilt
52 x 60-inches

Black Cat

Vintage Halloween decorations are back by popular demand. Showcase them on a crockery-filled shelf.

illow

18-inches square

Fabrics & Supplies

1/3 yard	**BEIGE FLORAL** for center square and checkerboard border
7 x 42-inch piece	**GREEN PRINT** for inner border
3/8 yard	**BLACK PRINT** for checkerboard border and cat/pumpkin appliqués
1 yard	**RED/BLACK HALLOWEEN PRINT** for outer border and pillow back
5-inch square	**GOLD PRINT** for center pumpkin appliqué
5 x 8-inch piece	**RED PRINT** for side pumpkin appliqués
1/4 yard	**BLACK PRINT** for binding

23-inch square of muslin lining for pillow top

quilt batting, at least 23-inches square

18-inch pillow form

template material

paper-backed fusible web for appliqué

pearl cotton or machine embroidery thread: black

tear-away fabric stabilizer (optional)

NOTE: read **Getting Started**, page 123, before beginning this project.

Pillow Top

Note: *The yardage given allows for the border strips to be cut on the crosswise grain. Read through **Border** instructions on pages 127–128 for general instructions on adding borders.*

Cutting

From **BEIGE FLORAL**:
- Cut 1, 9-1/2 x 42-inch strip. From the strip cut:
  1, 9-1/2-inch center square
  2, 1-1/2 x 26-inch strips

From **GREEN PRINT**:
- Cut 2, 2-1/2 x 42-inch inner border strips

From **BLACK PRINT**:
- Cut 1, 12 x 14-inch rectangle (set aside to be used for the cat and pumpkin face carving appliqués)
- Cut 2, 1-1/2 x 26-inch strips

From **RED/BLACK HALLOWEEN PRINT**:
- Cut 2, 2-1/2 x 42-inch outer border strips

Assembling and Attaching the Borders

Step 1 Attach the 2-1/2-inch wide **GREEN** inner border strips to the 9-1/2-inch **BEIGE FLORAL** center square. The appliqué can be done at this time, refer to **Fusible Web Appliqué** on page 15. The appliqué shapes are on pages 101-103.

Step 2 Aligning long edges, sew together a 1-1/2 x 26-inch **BEIGE** and **BLACK** strips; press. Make 2 strip sets. Cut the strip sets into segments.

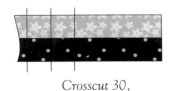

Crosscut 30,

1-1/2-inch wide segments

Step 3 Sew together 7 of the Step 2 segments. Remove 1 of the 1-1/2-inch **BLACK** squares; press. Make a total of 2 checkerboard border strips. <u>At this point each checkerboard border should measure 1-1/2 x 13-1/2-inches.</u> Sew the checkerboard borders to the top/bottom edges of the pillow center.

Step 4 Sew together 8 of the Step 2 segments. Remove 1 of the 1-1/2-inch **BEIGE** squares; press. Make a total of 2 checkerboard border strips. <u>At this point each checkerboard border should measure 1-1/2 x 15-1/2-inches.</u> Sew the checkerboard borders to the side edges of the pillow center.

Step 5 Attach the 2-1/2-inch wide **RED/BLACK HALLOWEEN PRINT** outer border strips.

Putting It All Together

Layer the 23-inch muslin lining square, batting square, and pillow top. Baste the layers together and quilt as desired. Refer to **Finishing the Quilt** on page 128 for complete instructions.

Pillow Back

Cutting

From RED/BLACK HALLOWEEN PRINT:
• Cut 2, 19-1/2 x 25-inch pillow back rectangles

Assembling the Pillow Back

Step 1 With wrong sides together, fold each 19-1/2 x 25-inch **RED/BLACK HALLOWEEN PRINT** pillow back rectangle in half crosswise to make 2,

12-1/2 x 19-1/2-inch double-thick pillow back pieces. Overlap the 2 folded edges so the pillow back measures 19-1/2-inches square. Pin the pieces together and stitch around the entire piece to create a single pillow back; use a scant 1/4-inch seam allowance. The double thickness of each back piece will make the pillow back more stable and give it a nice finishing touch.

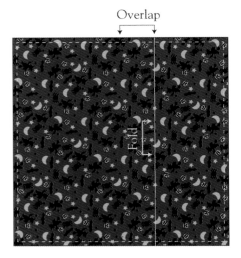

Overlap

Fold

Step 2 With wrong sides together, layer the pillow back and the pillow top; pin. Stitch around the outside edges; use a scant 1/2-inch seam allowance.

Binding

Cutting

From BLACK PRINT:
• Cut 2, 3-1/2 x 42-inch strips

Sew the binding to the quilt using a 1/2-inch seam allowance. This measurement will produce a 5/8-inch wide finished double binding. Refer to **Binding** and **Diagonal Piecing** on page 128 for complete instructions.

Pumpkin

*Trace 2 onto
fusible web*

Pumpkin

*Trace 1 onto
fusible web*

Pumpkin Face

*Trace 1 each onto
fusible web*

Pattern Notes

Appliqué Pieces

*The appliqué shapes are reversed for tracing
purposes. When the appliqué is finished,
it will appear as it does in the pillow diagram.*

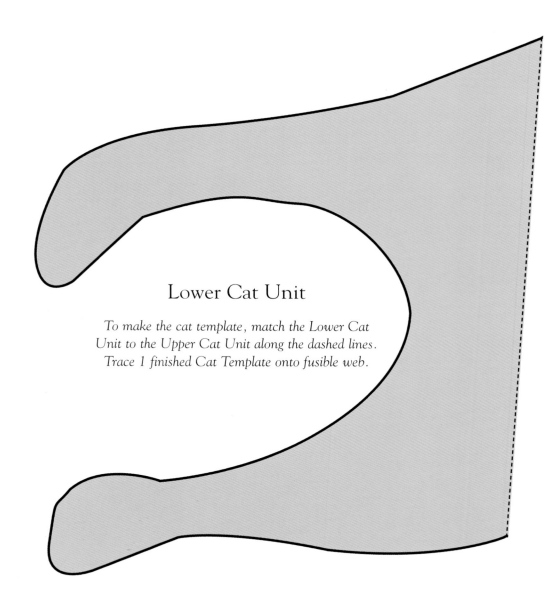

Lower Cat Unit

*To make the cat template, match the Lower Cat
Unit to the Upper Cat Unit along the dashed lines.
Trace 1 finished Cat Template onto fusible web.*

Pattern Notes

Appliqué Pieces

The appliqué shapes are reversed for tracing purposes. When the appliqué is finished, it will appear as it does in the pillow diagram.

Upper Cat Unit

To make the cat template, match the Lower Cat Unit to the Upper Cat Unit along the dashed lines. Trace 1 finished Cat Template onto fusible web.

Black Cat Pillow
18-inches square

Quick Tricks

For small-scale decorating, display antique collectible candles in a fun-filled doll cupboard.

Table Runner

22 x 44-inches

Fabrics & Supplies

1/2 yard   **BLACK PRINT** for pinwheel blocks and inner border

1/3 yard   **COCOA PRINT** for pinwheel blocks

1/2 yard   **RED PRINT** for side and corner triangles

1/2 yard   **RED/BLACK HALLOWEEN PRINT** for outer border

3/8 yard   **BLACK PRINT** for binding

1-3/8 yards for backing

quilt batting, at least 28 x 50-inches

NOTE: read **Getting Started**, *page 123, before beginning this project.*

Pinwheel Blocks

Makes 3 large blocks
Makes 4 small corner blocks

Cutting

From **BLACK PRINT**:
- Cut 1, 4-7/8 x 42-inch strip
- Cut 1, 2-7/8 x 42-inch strip

From **COCOA PRINT**:
- Cut 1, 4-7/8 x 42-inch strip
- Cut 1, 2-7/8 x 42-inch strip

Piecing

Step 1   With right sides together, layer the 4-7/8 x 42-inch **BLACK** and **COCOA** strips. Press together, but do not sew. Cut the layered strips into squares. Cut the squares in half diagonally to make 12 sets of triangles. Stitch 1/4-inch from the diagonal edge of each pair of triangles; press. <u>At this point each triangle-pieced square should measure 4-1/2-inches square.</u>

Crosscut 6, 4-7/8-inch squares

Make 12, 4-1/2-inch triangle-pieced squares

Step 2 Sew the triangle-pieced squares together in pairs; press. Sew the pairs together to make the pinwheel blocks; press. <u>At this point each large pinwheel block should measure 8-1/2-inches square.</u>

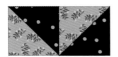

Make 6

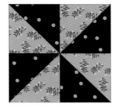

Make 3 large pinwheels

Step 3 With right sides together, layer the 2-7/8 x 42-inch **BLACK** and **COCOA** strips. Press together, but do not sew. Cut the layered strips into squares. Cut the squares in half diagonally to make 16 sets of triangles. Stitch 1/4-inch from the diagonal edge of each pair of triangles; press. <u>At this point each triangle-pieced square should measure 2-1/2-inches square.</u>

Crosscut 8, 2-7/8-inch squares

Make 16, 2-1/2-inch triangle-pieced squares

Step 4 Sew the triangle-pieced squares together in pairs; press. Sew the pairs together to make the pinwheel blocks; press. <u>At this point each pinwheel corner block should measure 4-1/2-inches square.</u> Set the corner blocks aside to be used in the border.

Make 8

Make 4 pinwheel corner blocks

Quilt Center

Note: *The side and corner triangles are larger than necessary and will be trimmed before the borders are added.*

Cutting

From **RED PRINT:**
- Cut 1, 13 x 42-inch strip. From the strip cut:
  1, 13-inch square. Cut the square diagonally into quarters to make 4 side triangles.
  2, 8-inch squares. Cut the squares in half diagonally to make 4 corner triangles.

Quilt Center Assembly

Step 1 Referring to the quilt center assembly diagram, sew together the 3 large pinwheel blocks and the **RED** side triangles. Press the seam allowances toward the side triangles.

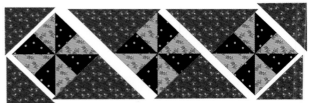

Quilt Center Assembly Diagram

Step 2 Pin the rows together at the block intersections and sew the rows together; press.

Step 3 Sew the **RED** corner triangles to the quilt center; press.

Step 4 Trim away the excess fabric from the side and corner triangles taking care to allow a 1/4-inch seam allowance beyond the corners of each block. Refer to **Trimming Side and Corner Triangles** on pages 125–126 for complete instructions.

Borders

Note: *The yardage given allows for the border strips to be cut on the crosswise grain. Read through **Border** instructions on pages 127–128 for general instructions on adding borders.*

Cutting

From **BLACK PRINT:**
- Cut 3, 1-1/2 x 42-inch inner border strips

From **RED/BLACK HALLOWEEN PRINT:**
• Cut 3, 4-1/2 x 42-inch outer border strips

Attaching the Borders

Step 1 Attach the 1-1/2-inch wide **BLACK** inner border strips.

Step 2 Attach the 4-1/2-inch wide **RED/BLACK HALLOWEEN PRINT** top/bottom outer border strips.

Step 3 For the side outer borders measure just the quilt top including seam allowances, but not the top/bottom borders. Cut the 4-1/2-inch wide **RED/BLACK HALLOWEEN PRINT** side outer border strips to this length. Sew a 4-1/2-inch pinwheel corner block to both ends of the border strips; press. Sew the border strips to the side edges of the runner center; press.

Putting It All Together

Trim the backing and batting so they are 6-inches larger than the runner top. Refer to **Finishing the Quilt** on page 128 for complete instructions.

Binding

Cutting

From **BLACK PRINT:**
• Cut 4, 2-3/4 x 42-inch strips

Sew the binding to the quilt using a 3/8-inch seam allowance. This measurement will produce a 1/2-inch wide finished double binding. Refer to **Binding** and **Diagonal Piecing** on page 128 for complete instructions.

Quick Tricks Table Runner
22 x 44-inches

Fright Night

Celebrate the mystery and magic of Halloween with vintage dishes and fun fright-night memorabilia.

Table Square

42-inches square

Fabrics & Supplies

1/2 yard	**RED PRINT** for Block A
1/4 yard	**GOLD FLORAL** for Block A
3/4 yard	**BEIGE PRINT** for background
7/8 yard	**RED w/GOLD LEAF PRINT** for Block B and outer border
1/4 yard	**GREEN PRINT** for Block B
1/4 yard	**BLACK PRINT** for inner border
1/2 yard	**BLACK PRINT** for binding

2-2/3 yards for backing

quilt batting, at least 48-inches square

NOTE: read **Getting Started**, page 123, before beginning this project.

Block A

Makes 5 blocks

Cutting

From **RED PRINT:**
- Cut 5, 2-1/2 x 42-inch strips.
  From 1 of the strips cut:
  1, 2-1/2 x 20-inch strip

From **GOLD FLORAL:**
- Cut 2, 2-1/2 x 42-inch strips.
  From 1 of the strips cut:
  2, 2-1/2 x 20-inch strips

From **BEIGE PRINT:**
- Cut 6, 2-1/2 x 42-inch strips.
  From 1 of the strips cut:
  2, 2-1/2 x 20-inch strips

Piecing

Step 1   Aligning long edges sew together 2 of the 2-1/2 x 42-inch **RED** strips, 2 of the 2-1/2 x 42-inch **BEIGE** strips, and the 2-1/2 x 42-inch **GOLD FLORAL** strip. Press the strip set referring to **Hints and Helps for Pressing Strip Sets** on page 111. Cut the strip set into segments.

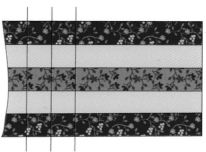

Crosscut 10, 2-1/2-inch wide segments

Step 2 Aligning long edges sew together 2 of the 2-1/2 x 42-inch **RED** strips, and 3 of the 2-1/2 x 42-inch **BEIGE** strips; press. Cut the strip set into segments.

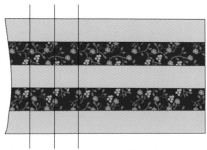

Crosscut 10, 2-1/2-inch wide segments

Step 3 Aligning long edges sew together the 2-1/2 x 20-inch **RED** strip, 2 of the 2-1/2 x 20-inch **BEIGE** strips, and 2 of the 2-1/2 x 20-inch **GOLD FLORAL** strips; press. Cut the strip set into segments.

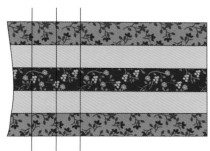

Crosscut 5, 2-1/2-inch wide segments

Step 4 Sew together the Step 1, 2, and 3 segments to make Block A; press. <u>At this point each Block A should measure 10-1/2-inches square.</u>

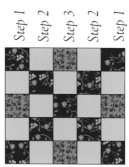

Block A   Make 5

Block B

Makes 4 blocks

Cutting

From **RED w/GOLD LEAF PRINT:**
- Cut 1, 6-1/2 x 42-inch strip. From the strip cut: 4, 6-1/2-inch squares

From **GREEN PRINT:**
- Cut 2, 2-7/8 x 42-inch strips

From **BEIGE PRINT:**
- Cut 2, 2-7/8 x 42-inch strips
- Cut 1, 2-1/2 x 42-inch strip. From the strip cut: 16, 2-1/2-inch squares

Piecing

Step 1 With right sides together, layer the 2-7/8 x 42-inch **GREEN** and **BEIGE** strips in pairs. Press together, but do not sew. Cut the layered strips into squares. Cut the squares in half diagonally to make 48 sets of triangles. Stitch 1/4-inch from the diagonal edge of each pair of triangles; press. <u>At this point each triangle-pieced square should measure 2-1/2-inches square.</u>

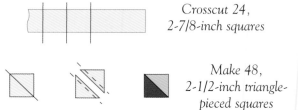

Crosscut 24, 2-7/8-inch squares

Make 48, 2-1/2-inch triangle-pieced squares

Step 2 Referring to the diagrams on page 111 for color placement, sew 3 of the triangle-pieced squares together; press. Make 8 top/bottom sawtooth units and 8 side sawtooth units. Sew 2 of the top/bottom sawtooth units to the edges of each 6-1/2-inch **RED w/GOLD LEAF PRINT** square; press. Sew 2-1/2-inch **BEIGE** squares to both ends of the remaining side sawtooth units; press. Sew the units to the side edges of each **RED w/GOLD LEAF PRINT** square unit; press. <u>At this point each Block B should measure 10-1/2-inches square.</u>

Make 8 top/bottom
sawtooth units

Make 8 side
sawtooth units

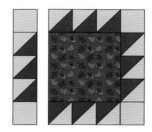
Make 4, Block B

Quilt Center

Quilt Center Assembly

Step 1 Referring to the quilt diagram for block placement, sew the A and B Blocks together in 3 rows of 3 blocks each. Press the seam allowances toward the A Blocks so the seams will fit snugly together with less bulk.

Step 2 Pin the rows together at the block intersections; sew the rows together. Press the seam allowances in one direction.

Borders

Note: *The yardage given allows for the border strips to be cut on the crosswise grain. Read through* **Border** *instructions on pages 127–128 for general instructions on adding borders.*

Cutting

From **BLACK PRINT:**
• Cut 4, 1-1/2 x 42-inch inner border strips

From **RED w/GOLD LEAF PRINT:**
• Cut 4, 5-1/2 x 43-inch outer border strips

Attaching the Borders

Step 1 Attach the 1-1/2-inch wide **BLACK** inner border strips.

Step 2 Attach the 5-1/2-inch wide **RED w/GOLD LEAF PRINT** outer border strips.

Putting It All Together

Cut the 2-2/3 yard length of backing fabric in half crosswise to make 2, 1-1/3 yard lengths. Refer to **Finishing the Quilt** on page 128 for complete instructions.

Binding

Cutting

From **BLACK PRINT:**
• Cut 5, 2-3/4 x 42-inch strips

Sew the binding to the quilt using a 3/8-inch seam allowance. This measurement will produce a 1/2-inch wide finished double binding. Refer to **Binding** and **Diagonal Piecing** on page 128 for complete instructions.

Hints and Helps for Pressing Strip Sets

When sewing strips of fabric together for strips sets, it is important to press the seam allowances nice and flat, usually to the dark fabric. Be careful not to stretch as you press, causing a "rainbow effect." This will affect the accuracy and shape of the pieces cut from the strip set. Press on the wrong side first with the strips perpendicular to the ironing board. Flip the piece over and press on the right side to prevent little pleats from forming at the seams. Laying the strip set lengthwise on the ironing board seems to encourage the rainbow effect.

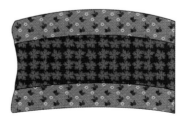

"Avoid this rainbow effect"

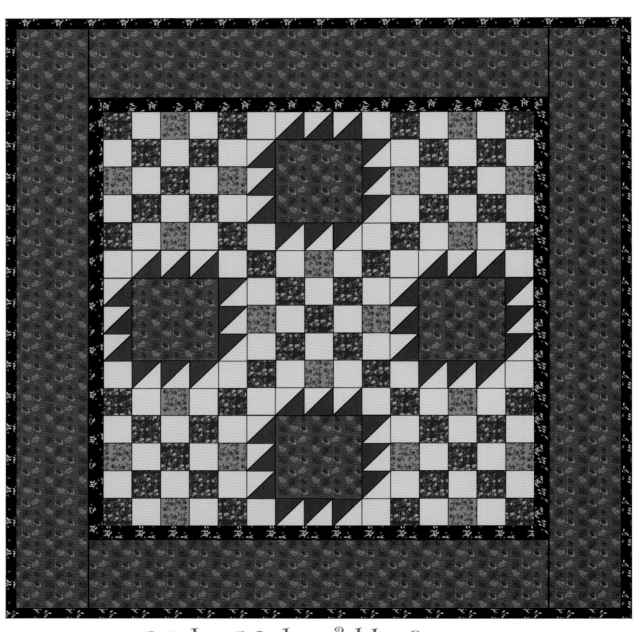

Fright Night Table Square

42-inches square

Tangle-toothed Jack-o-lanterns, displayed amid leafy tree branches, appear to have the last laugh at old Jack Frost.

Halloween Stars

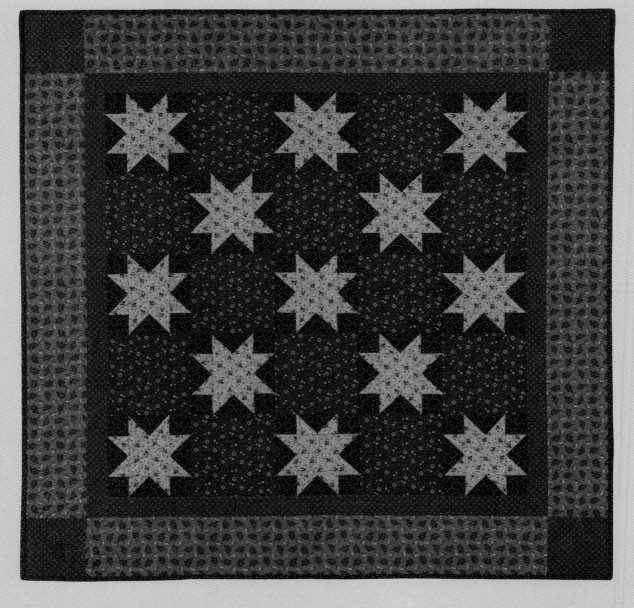

For a harvest of stars, the name of the game is Halloween Stars.

Wall Quilt

56-inches square

Fabrics & Supplies

7/8 yard   **GOLD PRINT** for star blocks

7/8 yard   **BLACK PRINT** for star blocks

7/8 yard   **RED FLORAL** for alternate blocks

5/8 yard   **GREEN PRINT** for inner border and corner blocks

1 yard   **GOLD/BROWN LEAF PRINT** for outer border

5/8 yard   **BLACK PRINT** for binding

3-1/2 yards for backing

quilt batting, at least 62-inches square

*NOTE: read **Getting Started**, page 123, before beginning this project.*

Star Blocks

Makes 13 blocks

Cutting

From **GOLD PRINT:**
- Cut 2, 4-1/2 x 42-inch strips.
  From the strips cut:
  13, 4-1/2-inch squares
- Cut 7, 2-1/2 x 42-inch strips.
  From the strips cut:
  104, 2-1/2-inch squares

From **BLACK PRINT:**
- Cut 10, 2-1/2 x 42-inch strips.
  From the strips cut:
  52, 2-1/2 x 4-1/2-inch rectangles
  52, 2-1/2-inch squares

Piecing

Step 1   With right sides together, position a 2-1/2-inch **GOLD** square on the corner of a 2-1/2 x 4-1/2-inch **BLACK** rectangle. Draw a diagonal line on the square and stitch on the line. Trim the seam allowance to 1/4-inch; press. Repeat this process at the opposite corner of the rectangle to make a star point unit.

Make 52

Step 2 Sew Step 1 star point units to the top/bottom edges of the 4-1/2-inch **GOLD** squares; press. Sew 2-1/2-inch **BLACK** squares to both ends of the remaining star point units; press. Sew the units to the side edges of each **GOLD** square unit; press. <u>At this point each star block should measure 8-1/2-inches square.</u>

Make 13

Quilt Center

Cutting

From **RED FLORAL**:
- Cut 3, 8-1/2 x 42-inch strips.
  From the strips cut:
  12, 8-1/2-inch alternate block squares

Quilt Center Assembly

Step 1 Referring to the quilt diagram for block placement, sew the star blocks and alternate blocks together in 5 rows of 5 blocks each. Press the seam allowances toward the alternate blocks so the seams will fit snugly together with less bulk.

Step 2 Pin the rows together at the block intersections and sew the rows together. Press the seam allowances in one direction.

Borders

*Note: The yardage given allows for the border strips to be cut on the crosswise grain. Diagonally piece the strips as needed, referring to **Diagonal Piecing** instructions on page 128. Read through **Border** instructions on pages 127–128 for general instructions on adding borders.*

Cutting

From **GREEN PRINT**:
- Cut 1, 6-1/2 x 42-inch strip. From the strip cut: 4, 6-1/2-inch corner squares
- Cut 5, 2-1/2 x 42-inch inner border strips

From **GOLD/BROWN LEAF PRINT**:
- Cut 5, 6-1/2 x 42-inch outer border strips

Attaching the Borders

Step 1 Attach the 2-1/2-inch wide **GREEN** inner border strips.

Step 2 Attach the 6-1/2-inch wide **GOLD/BROWN LEAF PRINT** top/bottom outer border strips.

Step 3 For the side outer borders, measure just the quilt top including seam allowances, but not the top/bottom borders. Cut the 6-1/2-inch wide **GOLD/BROWN LEAF PRINT** side outer border strips to this length. Sew a 6-1/2-inch **GREEN** corner square to both ends of the border strips; press. Sew the border strips to the side edges of the quilt center; press.

Putting It All Together

Cut the 3-1/2 yard length of backing fabric in half crosswise to make 2, 1-3/4 yard lengths. Refer to **Finishing the Quilt** on page 128 for complete instructions.

Binding

Cutting

From **BLACK PRINT**:
- Cut 6, 2-3/4 x 42-inch strips

Sew the binding to the quilt using a 3/8-inch seam allowance. This measurement will produce a 1/2-inch wide finished double binding. Refer to **Binding** and **Diagonal Piecing** on page 128 for complete instructions.

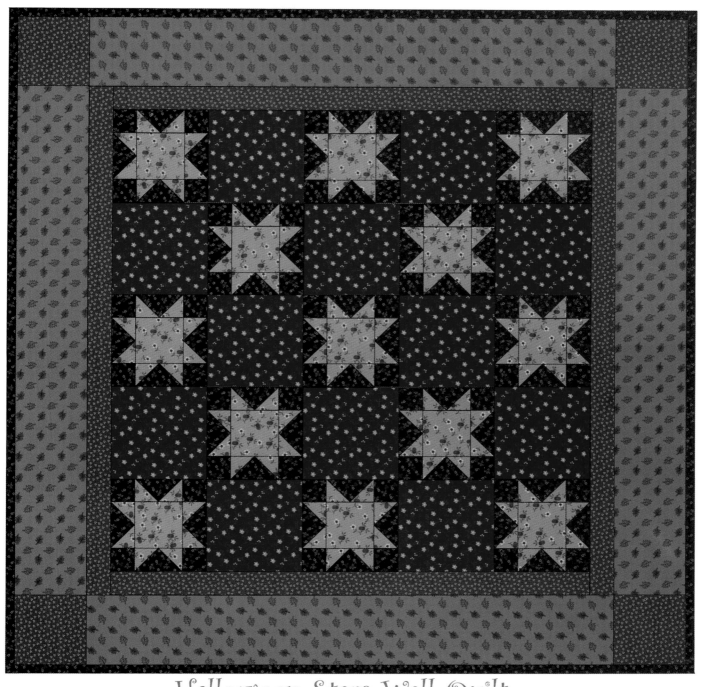

Halloween Stars Wall Quilt
56-inches square

Night Magic

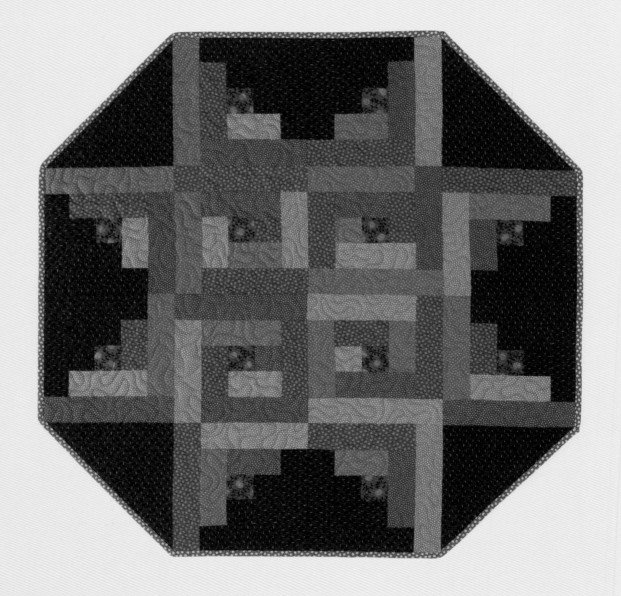

Set an elegant harvest table by accenting sage, cream and black with glistening amber—nature's gold.

Table Topper

40-inches in diameter

Fabrics & Supplies

1/8 yard   **ORANGE PUMPKIN PRINT** for center squares

1/4 yard   *each* of **4 ASSORTED ORANGE/GOLD PRINTS** for log cabin strips

7/8 yard   **BLACK PRINT** for log cabin strips and side triangles

1/2 yard   **GREEN FLORAL** for binding

1-1/4 yards for backing

quilt batting, at least 44-inches in diameter

NOTE: read **Getting Started**, *page 123, before beginning this project.*

Log Cabin Blocks

The Log Cabin block is the only block used in this table topper. To achieve the correct design, some blocks are assembled in a clockwise direction and some are assembled in a counterclockwise direction.

Cutting

From **ORANGE PUMPKIN PRINT:**
• Cut 1, 2-1/2 x 42-inch strip. From the strip cut: 12, 2-1/2-inch squares

From **ASSORTED ORANGE/GOLD PRINTS:**
• Cut a total of 12, 2-1/2 x 42-inch strips

From **BLACK PRINT:**
• Cut 5, 2-1/2 x 42-inch strips. From 1 of the strips cut: 8, 2-1/2-inch squares

BLOCK A
(assembled in a clockwise direction)

Makes 4 blocks

Piecing

Step 1   Sew a 2-1/2-inch wide **ASSORTED ORANGE/GOLD PRINT** strip to the right edge of a 2-1/2-inch **ORANGE PUMPKIN PRINT** square. Press the seam allowances toward the strip just added. Trim the strip even with the edges of the square.

Trim

Make 4

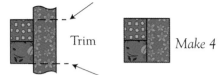

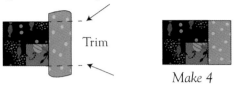

Step 2 Turn the Step 1 unit a quarter turn to the left and sew a 2-1/2-inch wide **ASSORTED ORANGE/GOLD PRINT** strip to the right edge of the 2-piece unit; press and trim.

Trim

Make 4

Step 3 Turn the Step 2 unit a quarter turn to the left and sew a 2-1/2-inch wide **ASSORTED ORANGE/GOLD PRINT** strip to the right edge of the unit; press and trim.

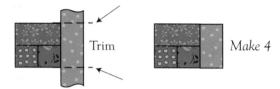

Trim

Make 4

Step 4 Working clockwise around the center square and referring to the diagram for color placement, continue adding the 2-1/2-inch wide **ASSORTED ORANGE/ GOLD PRINT** strips to complete Block A. Press and trim each strip before adding the next. Each Log Cabin block should measure 10-1/2-inches square. Adjust the seam allowances if needed.

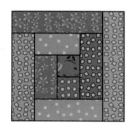

Block A
Make 4

BLOCK B
(assembled in a clockwise direction)

Makes 4 blocks

Piecing

Step 1 Sew together a 2-1/2-inch **ORANGE PUMPKIN PRINT** square and a 2-1/2-inch **BLACK** square. Turn the unit a quarter turn to the left and sew a 2-1/2-inch wide **BLACK** strip to the right edge of the 2-piece unit; press and trim.

Trim

Make 4

Step 2 Turn the Step 1 unit a quarter turn to the left and sew a 2-1/2-inch wide **ASSORTED ORANGE/GOLD PRINT** strip to the right edge of the unit; press and trim.

Trim

Make 4

Step 3 Turn the Step 2 unit a quarter turn to the left and sew a 2-1/2-inch wide **ASSORTED ORANGE/GOLD PRINT** strip to the right edge of the unit; press and trim.

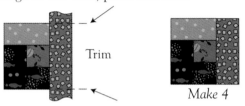

Trim

Make 4

Step 4 Working clockwise around the center square and referring to the block diagram for color placement, continue adding the 2-1/2-inch wide **ASSORTED ORANGE/GOLD PRINT STRIPS** and the **BLACK** strips to complete Block B. Press and trim each strip before adding the next. Each Log Cabin block should measure 10-1/2-inches square. Adjust the seam allowances if needed.

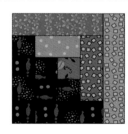

Block B
Make 4

BLOCK C
(assembled in a counterclockwise direction)

Makes 4 blocks

Piecing

Step 1 Sew together a 2-1/2-inch **ORANGE PUMPKIN PRINT** square and a 2-1/2-inch **BLACK** square; press. Turn the unit a quarter turn to the right and sew a 2-1/2-inch wide **BLACK** strip to the right edge of the 2-piece unit; press and trim.

Trim

Make 4

Step 2 Turn the Step 1 unit a quarter turn to the right and sew a 2-1/2-inch wide **ASSORTED ORANGE/ GOLD PRINT** strip to the right edge of the unit; press and trim.

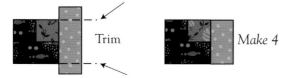

Trim   Make 4

Step 3 Turn the Step 2 unit a quarter turn to the right and sew a 2-1/2-inch wide **ASSORTED ORANGE/ GOLD PRINT** strip to the right edge of the unit; press and trim.

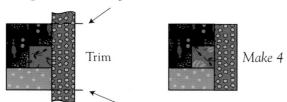

Trim   Make 4

Step 4 Working counterclockwise around the center square and referring to the block diagram for color placement, continue adding the 2-1/2-inch wide assorted **ORANGE/GOLD PRINT** strips and the **BLACK** strips to complete Block C. Press and trim each strip before adding the next. Each Log Cabin block should measure 10-1/2-inches square. Adjust the seam allowances if needed.

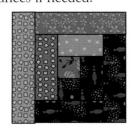

Block C
Make 4

Quilt Center

Note: *The side triangles are larger than necessary and will be trimmed before the project is quilted.*

Cutting

From **BLACK PRINT:**
- Cut 1, 16-inch square. Cut the square diagonally into quarters to make 4 side triangles.

Quilt Center Assembly

Step 1 Referring to the quilt assembly diagram for block placement, sew the A, B, and C Blocks and the **BLACK** side triangles

together in 4 rows of 4 units each. Press the seam allowances in alternating directions by rows so the seams will fit snugly together with less bulk.

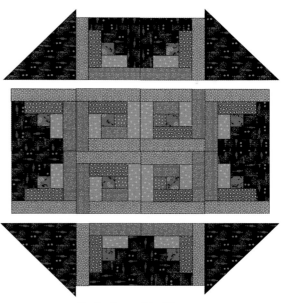

Quilt Assembly Diagram

Step 2 Pin the rows together at the block intersections and sew the rows together; press.

Step 3 Refer to **Trimming Black Side Triangles** to trim away the excess fabric from the **BLACK** side triangles.

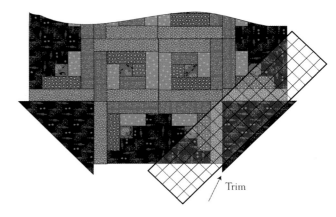

Trim

Trimming Black Side Triangles
Position your ruler on the quilt top and trim away the excess side triangle fabric.

Putting It All Together

Trim the backing and batting so they are 4-inches larger than the quilt top. Refer to **Finishing the Quilt** on page 128 for complete instructions.

Binding

Cutting

From **GREEN FLORAL:**

- Cut 5, 2-3/4 x 42-inch strips

Sew the binding to the quilt using a 3/8-inch seam allowance. This measurement will produce a 1/2-inch wide finished double binding. Refer to **Binding** and **Diagonal Piecing** on page 128 for complete instructions.

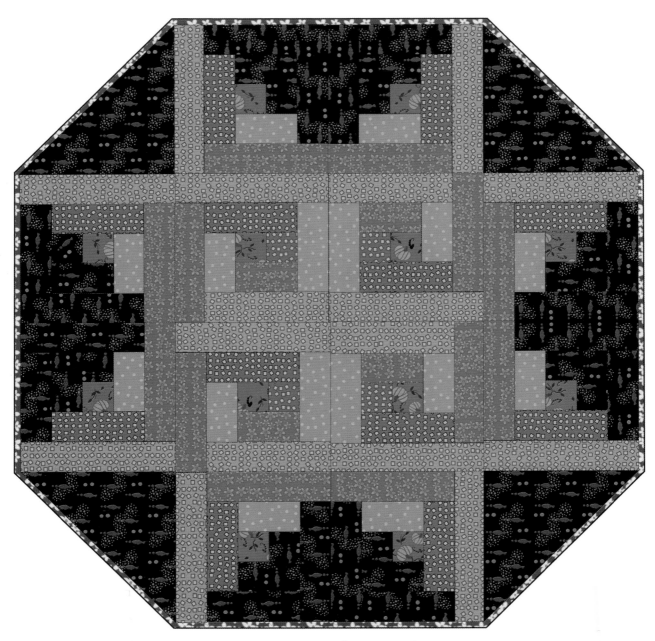

Night Magic Table Topper
40-inches in diameter

Getting Started

Yardage is based on 42-inch wide fabric. If your fabric is wider or narrower, it will affect the amount of necessary strips you need to cut in some patterns, and of course, it will affect the amount of fabric you have left over. Generally, Thimbleberries® patterns allow for a little extra fabric so you can confidently cut your pattern pieces with ease.

A rotary cutter, mat, and wide clear plastic ruler with 1/8-inch markings are needed tools in attaining accuracy. A beginner needs good tools just as an experienced quiltmaker needs good equipment. A 24 x 36-inch mat board is a good size to own. It will easily accommodate the average quilt fabrics and will aid in accurate cutting. The plastic ruler you purchase should be at least 6 x 24 inches and easy to read. Do not purchase a smaller ruler to save money. The large size will be invaluable to your quiltmaking success.

It is often recommended to prewash and press fabrics to test for colorfastness and possible shrinkage. If you choose to prewash, wash in cool water and dry in a cool to moderate dryer. Industry standards actually suggest that line drying is best. Shrinkage is generally very minimal and usually is not a concern. A good way to test your fabric for both shrinkage and colorfastness is to cut a 3-inch square of fabric. Soak the fabric in a white bowl filled with water. Squeeze the water out of the fabric and press it dry on a piece of muslin. If the fabric is going to release color, it will do so either in the water or when it is pressed dry. Remeasure the 3-inch fabric square to see if it has changed size considerably (more than

1/4- inch). If it has, wash, dry, and press the entire yardage. This little test could save you hours in prewashing and pressing.

Read instructions thoroughly before beginning a project. Each step will make more sense to you when you have a general overview of the whole process. Take one step at a time and follow the illustrations. They will often make more sense to you than the words. Take "baby steps" so you don't get overwhelmed by the entire process.

When working with flannel and other loosely woven fabrics, always prewash and dry. These fabrics almost always shrink more.

For piecing, place right sides of the fabric pieces together and use 1/4-inch seam allowances throughout the entire quilt unless otherwise specifically stated in the directions. An accurate seam allowance is the most important part of the quiltmaking process after accurately cutting. All the directions are based on accurate 1/4-inch seam allowances. It is very important to check your sewing machine to see what position your fabric should be to get accurate seams. To test, use a piece of 1/4-inch graph paper, stitch along the quarter inch line as if the paper were fabric. Make note of where the edge of the paper lines up with your presser foot or where it lines up on the throat of the plate of your machine. Many quilters place a piece of masking tape on the throat plate to help guide the edge of the fabric. Now test your seam allowance on fabric. Cut 2, 2-1/2-inch squares, place right sides together and stitch along one edge. Press seam allowances in one direction and measure. At this point the unit should measure 2-1/2 x 4-1/2-inches. If it does not, adjust your stitching guidelines and test again. Seam allowances are included in the cutting sizes given in this book.

Pressing is the third most important step in quiltmaking. As a general rule, you should never cross a stitched seam with another seam unless it has been pressed. Therefore, every time you stitch a seam, it needs to be pressed before adding another piece. Often, it will feel like you press as much as you sew, and often that is true. It is very important that you press and not iron the seams. Pressing is a firm, up-and-down motion that will flatten the seams but not distort the piecing. Ironing is a back-and-forth motion and will stretch and distort the small pieces. Most quilters use steam to help the pressing process. The moisture does help and will not distort the shapes as long as the pressing motion is used.

An old-fashioned rule is to press seam allowances in one direction, toward the darker fabric. Often, background fabrics are light in color and pressing toward the darker fabric prevents the seam allowances from showing through to the right side. Pressing seam allowances in one direction is thought to create a stronger seam. Also, for ease in hand-quilting, the quilting lines should fall on the side of the seam which is opposite the seam allowance. As you piece quilts, you will find these "rules" to be helpful but not neccesarily always appropriate. Sometimes seams need to be pressed in the opposite direction so the seams of different units will fit together more easily, which quilters refer to as seams "nesting" together. When sewing together two units with opposing seam allowances, use the tip of your seam ripper to gently guide the units under your presser foot. Sometimes it is necessary to re-press the seams to make the units fit together nicely. Always try to achieve the least bulk in one spot and accept that no matter which way you press, it may be a little tricky and it could be a little bulky.

Pressing Direction

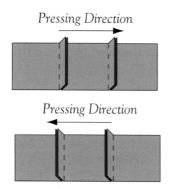

Pressing Direction

Squaring Up Blocks

To square up your blocks, first check the seam allowances. This is usually where the problem is, and it is always best to alter within the block rather than trim the outer edges. Next, make sure you have pressed accurately. Sometimes a block can become distorted by ironing instead of pressing.

To trim up block edges, use one of many clear plastic squares available on the market. Determine the center of the block; mark with a pin. Lay the square over the block and align as many perpendicular and horizontal lines as you can to the seams in your block. This will indicate where the block is off.

Do not trim all off on one side; this usually results in real distortion of the pieces in the block and the block design. Take a little off all sides until the block is square. When assembling many blocks, it is necessary to make sure *all* are the same size.

Tools and Equipment

Making beautiful quilts does not require a large number of specialized tools or expensive equipment. My list of favorites is short and sweet and includes the things I use over and over again because they are always accurate and dependable.

I find a long acrylic ruler indispensable for accurate rotary cutting. The ones I like most are an Omnigrid 6 x 24-inch grid acrylic ruler for cutting long strips and squaring up fabrics and quilt tops and a Masterpiece 45, 8 x 24-inch ruler for cutting 6- to 8-inch wide borders. I sometimes tape together two 6 x 24-inch acrylic rulers for cutting borders up to 12 inches wide.

A 15-inch Omnigrid square acrylic ruler is great for squaring up individual blocks and corners of a quilt top, for cutting strips up to 15 inches wide or long, and for trimming side and corner triangles.

I think the markings on my 23 x 35-inch Olfa rotary cutting mat stay visible longer than on other mats, and the lines are fine and accurate.

The largest size Olfa rotary cutter cuts through many layers of fabric easily, and it isn't cumbersome to use. The 2-1/2-inch blade slices through three layers of backing, batting, and a quilt top like butter.

An 8-inch pair of Gingher shears is great for cutting out appliqué templates and cutting fabric from a bolt or fabric scraps.

I keep a pair of 5-1/2-inch Gingher scissors by my sewing machine so it is handy for both machine work and handwork. This size is versatile and sharp enough to make large and small cuts equally well.

My Grabbit magnetic pin cushion has a surface that is large enough to hold a lot of straight pins and a strong magnet that keeps them securely in place.

Silk pins are long and thin, which means they won't leave large holes in your fabric. I like them because they increase accuracy in pinning pieces or blocks together and it is easy to press over silk pins as well.

For pressing individual pieces, blocks, and quilt tops, I use an 18 x 48-inch sheet of plywood covered with several layers of cotton fiberfill and topped with a layer of muslin stapled to the back. The 48-inch length allows me to press an entire width of fabric at one time without the need to reposition it, and the square ends are better than tapered ends on an ironing board for pressing finished quilt tops.

Rotary Cutting

SAFETY FIRST! The blades of a rotary cutter are very sharp and need to be for accurate cutting. Look at a variety of cutters to find one that feels good in your hand. All quality cutters have a safety mechanism to "close" the cutting blade when not in use. After each cut and before laying the rotary cutter down, close the blade. Soon this will become second nature to you and will prevent dangerous accidents. Always keep cutters out of the sight of children. Rotary cutters are very tempting to fiddle with when they are lying around. When your blade is dull or nicked, change it. Damaged blades do not cut accurately and require extra effort that can also result in slipping and injury. Also, always cut away from yourself for safety.

Fold the fabric in half lengthwise matching the selvage edges.

"Square off" the ends of your fabric before measuring and cutting pieces. This means that the cut edge of the fabric must be exactly perpendicular to the folded edge which creates a 90° angle. Align the folded and selvage edges of the fabric with the lines on the

6 x 24" ruler

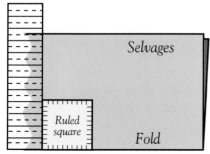

cutting board, and place a ruled square on the fold. Place a 6 x 24-inch ruler against the side of the square to get a 90° angle. Hold the ruler in place, remove the square, and cut along the edge of the ruler. If you are left-handed, work from the other end of the fabric. Use the lines on your cutting board to help line up fabric, but not to measure and cut strips. Use a ruler for accurate cutting, always checking to make sure your fabric is lined up with horizontal and vertical lines on the ruler.

Cutting Strips

When cutting strips or rectangles, cut on the crosswise grain. Strips can then be cut into squares or smaller rectangles.

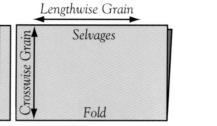

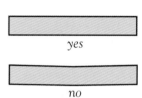

If your strips are not straight after cutting a few of them, refold the fabric, align the folded and selvage edges with the lines on the cutting board, and "square off" the edge again by trimming to straighten, and begin cutting.

Cutting Side and Corner Triangles

In projects with side and corner triangles, the instructions have you cut side and corner triangles larger than needed. This will allow you to square up the quilt and eliminates the frustration of ending up with pre-cut side and corner triangles that don't match the size of your pieced blocks.

To cut triangles, first cut squares. The project directions will tell you what size to make the squares and whether to cut them in half to make two triangles or to cut them in quarters to make four triangles, as shown in the diagrams. This cutting method will

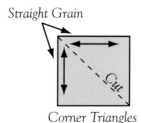

Corner Triangles

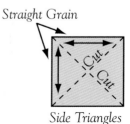

Side Triangles

give you side triangles that have the straight grain on the outside edges of the quilt. This is a very important part of quiltmaking that will help stabilize your quilt center.

Helpful Hints for Sewing with Flannel

Always prewash and machine dry flannel. This will prevent severe shrinkage after the quilt is made. Some flannels shrink more than others. For this reason, we have allowed approximately 1/4 yard extra for each fabric under the fabric requirements. Treat the more heavily napped side of solid flannels as the right side of the fabric.

Because flannel stretches more than other cotton calicos and because the nap makes them thicker, the quilt design should be simple. Let the fabric and color make the design statement.

Consider combining regular cotton calicos with flannels. The different textures complement each other nicely.

Use a 10 to 12 stitches per inch setting on your machine. A 1/4-inch seam allowance is also recommended for flannel piecing.

When sewing triangle-pieced squares together, take extra care not to stretch the diagonal seam. Trim off the points from the seam allowances to eliminate bulk.

Press gently to prevent stretching pieces out of shape.

Check block measurements as you progress. "Square up" the blocks as needed. Flannel will shift and it is easy to end up with blocks that are misshapen. If you trim and measure as you go, you are more likely to have accurate blocks. If you notice a piece of flannel is stretching more than the others, place it on the bottom when stitching on the machine. The natural action of the feed dogs will help prevent it from stretching.

Before stitching pieces, strips, or borders together, pin often to prevent fabric from stretching and moving. When stitching longer pieces together, divide the pieces into quarters and pin. Divide into even smaller sections to get more control.

Use a lightweight batting to prevent the quilt from becoming too heavy.

Cutting Triangles from Squares

Cutting accurate triangles can be intimidating for beginners, but a clear plastic ruler, rotary cutter, and cutting mat are all that are needed to make perfect triangles. The cutting instructions often direct you to cut strips, then squares, and then triangles.

Sewing Layered Strips Together

When you are instructed to layer strips, right sides together, and sew, you need to take some precautions. Gently lay a strip on top of another, carefully lining up the raw edges. Pressing the strips together will hold them together nicely, and a few pins here and there will also help. Be careful not to stretch the strips as you sew them together.

Rod Casing or Sleeve to Hang Quilts

To hang wall quilts, attach a casing that is made of the same fabric as the quilt back. Attach this casing at the top of the quilt, just below the binding. Often, it is helpful to attach a second casing at the bottom of the quilt so you can insert a dowel into it which will help weight the quilt and make it hang free of ripples.

To make a rod casing or "sleeve," cut enough strips of fabric equal to the width of the quilt plus 2 inches for side hems. Generally, 6-inch wide strips will accommodate most rods. If you are using a rod with a larger diameter, increase the width of the strips.

Seam the strips together to get the length needed; press. Fold the strip in half lengthwise, wrong sides together. Stitch the long raw edges together with a 1/4-inch seam allowance. Center the seam on the backside of the sleeve; press. The raw edges of the seam will be concealed when the sleeve is stitched to the back of the quilt. Turn under both of the short raw edges; press and stitch to hem the ends. The final measurement should be about 1/2 inch from the quilt edges.

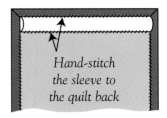

Hand-stitch the sleeve to the quilt back

Pin the sleeve to the back of the quilt so the top edge of the sleeve is just below the binding. Hand-stitch the top edge of the sleeve in place, then the bottom edge. Make sure to knot and secure your stitches at each end of the sleeve to make sure it will not pull away from the quilt with use. Slip the rod into the casing. If your wall quilt is not directional, making a sleeve for the bottom edge will allow you to turn your quilt end to end to relieve the stress at the top edge. You could also slip a dowel into the bottom sleeve to help anchor the lower edge of the wall quilt.

Choosing a Quilt Design

Quilting is such an individual process that it is difficult to recommend designs for each quilt. There are hundreds of quilting stencils available at quilt shops. (Templates are used generally for appliqué shapes; stencils are used for marking quilting designs.)

There are a few suggestions that may help you decide how to quilt your project, depending on how much time you would like to spend quilting. Many quilters now use professional long-arm quilting machines or hire someone skilled at running these machines to do the quilting. This, of course, frees up more time to piece.

Quilting Suggestions

Repeat one of the design elements in the quilt as part of the quilting design.

Two or three parallel rows of echo quilting outside an appliqué piece will highlight the shape.

Stipple or meander quilting behind a feather or central motif will make the primary design more prominent.

Look for quilting designs that will cover two or more borders, rather than choosing separate designs for each individual border.

Quilting in the ditch of seams is an effective way to get a project quilted without a great deal of time marking the quilt.

Marking the Quilting Design

When marking the quilt top, use a marking tool that will be visible on the quilt fabric and yet will be easy enough to remove. Always test your marking tool on a scrap of fabric before marking the entire quilt.

Along with a multitude of commercial marking tools available, you may find that very thin slivers of hand soap (Dial, Ivory, etc.) work really well for marking medium to dark color fabrics. The thin lines of soap show up nicely and they are easily removed by simply rubbing gently with a piece of like-colored fabric.

Hints and Helps for Pressing Strip Sets

Avoid this rainbow effect

When sewing strips of fabric together for strip sets, it is important to press the seam allowances nice and flat, usually to the darker fabric. Be careful not to stretch as you press, causing a "rainbow effect." This will affect the accuracy and shape of the pieces cut from the strip set. I like to press on the wrong side first and with the strips perpendicular to the ironing board. Then I flip the piece over and press on the right side to prevent little pleats from forming at the seams. Laying the strip set lengthwise on the ironing board seems to encourage the rainbow effect, as shown in the diagram.

Borders

NOTE: Cut borders to the width called for. Always cut border strips a few inches longer than needed, just to be safe. Diagonally piece the border strips together as needed.

1. With pins, mark the center points along all 4 sides of the quilt. For the top and bottom borders, measure the quilt from left to right through the middle.

2. Measure and mark the border lengths and center points on the strips cut for the borders before sewing them on.

Trim away excess fabric

3. Pin the border strips to the quilt and stitch a 1/4-inch seam. Press the seam allowances toward the border. Trim off excess border lengths.

4. For the side borders, measure your quilt from top to bottom, including the borders just added, to determine the length of the side borders.

5. Measure and mark the side border lengths as you did for the top and bottom borders.

6. Pin and stitch the side border strips in place. Press and trim the border strips even with the borders just added.

Trim away excess fabric

7. If your quilt has multiple borders, measure, mark, and sew additional borders to the quilt in the same manner.

Decorative Stitches

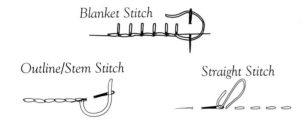

Blanket Stitch

Outline/Stem Stitch   *Straight Stitch*

Finishing the Quilt

1. Remove the selvages from the backing fabric. Sew the long edges together, and press. Trim the backing and batting so they are 4 inches to 6 inches larger than the quilt top.

2. Mark the quilt top for quilting. Layer the backing, batting, and quilt top. Baste the 3 layers together and quilt.

3. When quilting is complete, remove basting. Hand-baste all 3 layers together a scant 1/4 inch from the edge. This hand-basting keeps the layers from shifting and prevents puckers from forming when adding the binding. Trim excess batting and backing fabric even with the edge of the quilt top. Add the binding as shown at right.

Diagonal Piecing

Stitch diagonally   *Trim to 1/4-inch seam allowance*   *Press seam open*

Binding

1. Diagonally piece the binding strips. Fold the strip in half lengthwise, wrong sides together, and press.

Double-layer Binding

2. Unfold and trim one end at a 45° angle. Turn under the edge 3/8-inch and press. Refold the strip.

Fold line

3. With raw edges of the binding and quilt top even, stitch with a 3/8-inch seam allowance, starting 2 inches from the angled end.

4. Miter the binding at the corners. As you approach a corner of the quilt, stop sewing 3/8 inch from the corner of the quilt.

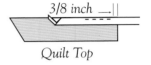

3/8 inch

Quilt Top

5. Clip the threads and remove the quilt from under the presser foot. Flip the binding strip up and away from the quilt, then fold the binding down even with the raw edge of the quilt. Begin sewing at the upper edge. Miter all 4 corners in this manner.

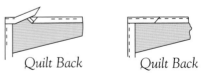

Quilt Top   *Quilt Top*

6. Trim the end of the binding so it can be tucked inside of the beginning binding about 1/2 inch. Finish stitching the seam.

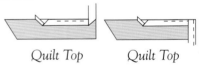

Quilt Back   *Quilt Back*

7. Turn the folded edge of the binding over the raw edges and to the back of the quilt so that the stitching line does not show. Hand-sew the binding in place, folding in the mitered corners as you stitch.

Quilt Back   *Quilt Back*   *Quilt Back*